Father Lee's Opera Quiz Book

Father Lee's

OPERA
QUIZ BOOK

M. OWEN LEE

UNIVERSITY OF TORONTO PRESS
Toronto Buffalo London

© University of Toronto Press Incorporated 2000
Toronto Buffalo London
Printed in Canada

ISBN 0-8020-8384-6

∞

Printed on acid-free paper

Canadian Cataloguing in Publication Data

Lee, M. Owen, 1930–
Father Lee's opera quiz book

ISBN 0-8020-8384-6

1. Opera – Miscellanea.   I. Title.   II. Title: Opera quiz book.

ML1700.L34 2000   782.1   C00-931140-8

The contents of this volume are reprinted with permission of the University of
North Carolina Press, Duke University Press, and Oxford University Press,
the successive publishers of *The Opera Quarterly*.

University of Toronto Press acknowledges the financial assistance to its publishing program
of the Canada Council for the Arts and the Ontario Arts Council.

University of Toronto Press acknowledges the financial support for its publishing activities of
the Government of Canada through the Book Publishing Industry Development Program
(BPIDP).

for
Iain Scott
master of operatic fact and lore

Contents

Acknowledgments

As each of the forty-four puzzles in this book has its own introduction, I need only say here that every definition in every puzzle is concerned with opera. There are no extinct Arabian birds or inactive Pacific volcanoes in the crosswords or double crostics to follow. All but the first two puzzles (the easiest ones) first appeared in *The Opera Quarterly*, and I should like to thank, once again, the four long-suffering editors who attended with patience and good humour to their first printing – Irene Sloan, Bruce Burroughs, William Ashbrook, and E. Thomas Glasow – as well as, for help given in various ways, Neylan Allebaugh, Brian Bailey, Richard Toporoski, Benjamin Torbert, and Guy Trudel.

I also owe a lasting debt of thanks to all the people associated with the Texaco Opera Quiz, which assembles during the intermissions of the Saturday afternoon live broadcasts from the Metropolitan Opera in New York. For the past eighteen years I have honed my quiz-maker's skills as panellist and occasional quizmaster during those tense but fun-filled sessions under the direction of Richard Mohr and Michael Bronson and their assistants Vinnie Volpe and Elaine Warner, and under the sponsorship of Michael Keenan and Diane Herzman. It would be invidious to single out any one of the more than fifty panellists with whom I served, but not one of them will object to my mentioning with special affection the wise and witty man who presided as quizmaster for most of those years, Edward Downes.

Finally, I must thank John St James, who first thought up the baseball section of the puzzle I have named 'Deconstruction in Dixie,' and who with diligence and with unfailing good spirits saw to the editing and preparation of the puzzles for this volume. And thanks as always to the good people at the University of Toronto Press – Suzanne Rancourt, Barbara Porter, and Kristen Pederson.

M. OWEN LEE

Cartoons on pages 53, 57, 61, 65, 95 by Melchiore Delfico.

Cartoons on pages 79, 83, 127, 145 by Enrico Caruso.

Cartoons on pages 107, 111, 137 by Rea Irvin.

ACT I

Quizzes

How Do You Solve a Problem Like ...?

Our first (and easiest) puzzle concerns itself with one of the most famous sopranos of the twentieth century. Use the alliterative descriptions of the heroines she has sung on stage and/or records to fill in the blanks. The initial letters of the eleven heroines' names will spell out the name of the famed soprano. A perfect score, with each blank correctly filled in, is 70. If you get 35, you're ready for the puzzles that follow.

Pretty (but poor) Parisian   _ _ _ _

Ardent African   _ _ _ _

Spunky Sevillian   _ _ _ _ _ _

Black Sea beauty   _ _ _ _ _ _ _ _ _

Swedish sweetheart   _ _ _ _ _ _ _

Seguidilla-singing seductress   _ _ _ _ _ _ _

Saddened sleepwalker   _ _ _ _ _ _

Maddened murderess   _ _ _ _ _ _

Iberian inamorata   _ _ _ _ _ _ _ _

Head-losing heroine   _ _ _ _
     _ _ _ _ _ _ _

Seduced Sicilian   _ _ _ _ _ _ _ _ _

Broadway Moments

Speaking of solving a problem like Maria, I suppose that even a non-opera-goer could suggest an operatic moment to match another Richard Rodgers song, 'Mimi,' and possibly a moment that suggests Ray Henderson's 'Don't Bring Lulu' as well. But can you think of a MOMENT (aria or otherwise) in opera to match the following songs, all of them written for the Broadway stage? A good score is ten out of fifteen. Broadway fans can score a possible forty-five by naming as well the COMPOSER of each Broadway song and the SHOW it comes from. One of our songs reaches back almost a hundred years, so, as Irving Berlin once said in a Broadway song, 'Let's Take an Old Fashioned Walk.'

1. 'Every Day Is Ladies Day with Me,' especially the line 'I never could find any fun in wasting all my time on one ...'

2. 'Fugue for Tinhorns,' especially the line 'I've got the horse right here ...'

3. 'Hernando's Hideaway,' especially the line 'All you hear are castanets ...'

4. 'I Feel Pretty,' especially the line 'I hardly can believe it's me ...'

5. 'I Hate Men,' especially the line 'Than ever marry one of them I'd rest a virgin rather ...'

6. 'I Love Louisa,' with the next line 'Louisa loves me ...'

7. 'The Man I Love,' especially the line 'Someday he'll come along ...'

8. 'Night and Day,' especially the line 'There's an Oh, such a hungry yearning, burning inside of me ...'

9. 'One More Kiss,' especially the line 'This one must be the last ...'

10. 'Out of My Dreams,' with the next line 'And into your arms I long to fly ...'

11. 'Send In the Clowns,' especially the line 'I thought that you'd want what I want ...'

12. 'The Touch of Your Hand,' especially the line 'You'll understand ...'

13. 'What Is This Thing Called Love?', especially the line 'Just who can solve its mystery ...'

14. 'Where's the Mate for Me?', especially the line 'Who cares if my boat goes upstream ...'

15. 'With a Song in My Heart,' especially the line 'At the sound of your voice heaven opens its portals to me ...'

Quotable Quotes

'Pigeons on the grass alas.' Opera librettos are full of such quotable quotes. For each of the twenty quotations that follow, you are invited to identify the SPEAKER and the OPERA. (Though the quotations may be less familiar than the 'Pigeons' spoken of by Saint Ignatius, the operas the quotations come from are all more familiar than *Four Saints in Three Acts*.) Give yourself a half point if you can name the opera but not the speaker. A casual operagoer should score five, a fan ten, a libretto freak nineteen or even twenty. Who said ...?

1. 'The cheese has dropped right onto the macaroni.' (*Sui maccheroni il cacio v'è cascato.*)

2. 'In the winter he likes them plump.' (*Vuol d'inverno la grassotta.*)

3. 'White is beautiful.' (*Weiss ist schön.*)

4. 'A girl ought to know where the devil has his tail.' (*Una donna ... dee saper ... dove il diavolo ha la coda.*)

5. 'We're not married, you know. I hate lovers who act like husbands.' (*All'altar non siamo uniti. Io detesto quegli amanti che la fanno da ... mariti.*)

6. 'A tempest in heaven, on earth a murder!' (*Una tempesta in cielo, in terra un omicidio!*)

7. 'Over the tower of horrors, Death himself seems to be poised on wings of darkness.' (*Sull'orrida torre, ahi, par che la morte con ali de tenebre librando si va.*)

8. 'I'll be waiting for you out there, behind the orchard.' (*Io v'aspetto qui fuori, dietro l'orto.*)

9. 'The gate of the orchard creaked, and a footstep rustled on the sand.' (*Stridea l'uscio dell'orto, e un passo sfiorava la rena.*)

10. 'Who was the woman I saw walking to the riverbank?' (*Wer war das Weib, das ich zum Ufer schreiten sah?*)

11. 'You ask if I hear it? If I hear the music? It's coming from inside me!' (*Ob ich nicht höre? Oh ich die Musik nicht höre? Sie kommt doch aus mir.*)

12. 'My baby touches the moon with his little finger.' (*Il mio bimbo … tocca la luna col suo ditino.*)

13. 'Does the elf know nothing of the Golden Eye that wakes and sleeps by turns?' (*Nichts weiss der Alp von des Goldes Auge, das wechselnd wacht und schläft?*)

14. 'You see, my son, time becomes space here.' (*Du sieh'st, mein Sohn, zum Raum wird hier die Zeit.*)

15. 'Put out the torches! Hide the moon! Hide the stars!' (*Löscht die Fackeln aus! Verbergt den Mond, verbergt die Sterne!*)

16. 'To the devil with America! She shall not go!' (*Al diavolo l'America! … Non partirà!*)

17. 'The bird that escapes from its cage often at night returns in desperate flight to beat its wings against the bars.' (*L'oiseau qui fuit ce qu'il croit l'esclavage, le plus souvent la nuit, d'un vol désespéré revient battre au vitrage.*)

18. 'In the midst of pleasure I long for pain.' (*Aus Freuden sehn ich mich nach Schmerzen.*)

19. 'If I were God, I would have pity on the human heart.' (*Si j'étais Dieu, j'aurais pitié du coeur des hommes.*)

20. 'We die not for ourselves alone, but for one another, sometimes even in the place of another. Who knows?' (*On ne meurt pas chacun pour soi, mais les uns pour les autres, ou même les uns à la place des autres, qui sait?*)

Please, Mr Postman

Each of the following bilingual quotations comes from an operatic letter. For the first six you are invited to name the SENDER and the RECEIVER of the letter in question. In each of the last ten, three people are involved – the third being somehow a PARTY to the reading or writing of the letter. So forty-two names constitute a perfect score. An opera fan should be able to come up with twenty names, an opera fanatic with thirty. Name all forty-two if you expect to be postmaster general. *RSVP.*

1. *Teneste la promessa* ... 'You have kept your promise. The duel took place. The baron was wounded but is recovering.'

2. *Ja k Vam pišu* ... 'I write to you – what more can I say? I know you have it in your power to treat me with contempt.'

3. *Kannst du eine Toilette von deiner Gnäd'gen annektieren* ... 'If you can appropriate a dress from your mistress and present yourself elegantly, I'll be glad to introduce you. Just get the time off.'

4. *O mon cher amant, je te jure* ... 'O my dear love, I swear that I love you with all my heart. But, really, this poverty is too hard to bear.'

5. *Nel dì della vittoria* ... 'I met them on the day of my victory, and I was astonished at the things I heard from them.'

6. *Prenez patience, l'heure est prochaine* ... 'Have patience, the hour is near. Write again to my father. If he gives a final refusal, I promise to elope with you.'

7. *La femme que je te conseillerais de choisir* ... 'The wife I would advise you to choose is the very one who brings you my letter.'

8. *Per la memoria che ci lega* ... 'By the memory that binds us, in the name of the past so dear to me, I pray you, trust this man.'

9. *Amico, cercherete quel bel fior di fanciulla* ... 'My friend, go and see that sweet flower of a girl. Since that happy time, three years have passed.'

10. *La tua sposa ... stanotte in mar ti fuggirà* ... 'Your wife will escape tonight by sea aboard a Dalmatian brigantine.'

11. *Le troisième soir qui suivra cette lettre* ... 'On the third night that follows your receipt of this letter, light a lamp at the top of the tower that looks on the sea.'

12. *Sei la gaia comare* ... 'You are the merry wife, the merry groom am I, and between the two of us we can make a pair.'

13. *Le vostre assidue premure hanno eccitata la mia curiosità* ... 'Your diligent attentions have aroused my curiosity. My guardian is leaving the house today. As soon as he's gone, find some way to tell me your name, your rank, and your intentions.'

14. *Che soave zefiretto* ... 'What a sweet little breeze will be sighing tonight among the pine trees in the grove!'

15. *Elle eut hier seize ans* ... 'Yesterday she turned sixteen. Everything about her charms – her beauty, her youth, her grace.'

16. *Stasera alle undici* ... 'This evening at eleven, in the usual villa by the Seine, for an affair of great political significance.'

Opera in Paris

The Parisian playwright Eugène Scribe decided, after writing some 350 plays and libretti, to cover all the alphabet letters in his titles. X and Y were the toughies. But he came up with *Xacarilla* and *Yvonne*. This quiz invites you, similarly, to name, for each letter of the alphabet, an OPERA that is set at least partly in PARIS. You are given four clues for each entry – the initial letter of the opera's title (discounting articles), a headline description of its plot, its composer, and its date. Standard works set in Paris (*Andrea Chénier*, *La Bohème*, *Dialogues des Carmélites*, *Louise*, *Lulu*, *Manon*, *Manon Lescaut*, *Il Tabarro*, and *La Traviata*) have been bypassed for less familiar fare. In three cases English titles are required. And, Paris being Paris, a couple of light operas are included. Your quizmaster hasn't found any Parisian titles beginning with those toughies X and Y. If you can come up with any, you'll be ready to take over his job. Meanwhile, as Massenet's lovers sing, 'À Paris!'

A. STAR OF COMÉDIE-FRANÇAISE POISONED BY RIVAL!
   (Cilea, 1902)

B. MANON AND DES GRIEUX MEET IN TWENTIETH CENTURY!
   (Henze, 1951)

C. GOLDSMITH COMMITS SERIAL MURDERS TO RECOVER OWN CREATIONS!
   (Hindemith, 1926)

D. HIGH-MINDED REVOLUTIONARY CLASHES WITH EXTREMIST RIVAL!
   (Eaton, 1978)

E. GYPSY GIRL RESCUED BY CATHEDRAL BELL RINGER!
   (Dargomyzhsky, 1847)

F. RUSSIAN PRINCESS FALLS FOR HUSBAND'S MURDERER!
   (Giordano, 1898)

G. BEAUMARCHAIS & CO. SAVE MARIE ANTOINETTE FROM GUILLOTINE!
   (Corigliano, 1991)

H. 24 AUGUST 1572 – A DAY THAT WILL LIVE IN INFAMY!
   (Meyerbeer, 1836)

I. BRIDEGROOM'S HORSE EATS IRREPLACEABLE HAT!
    (Rota, 1955)

J. JAZZ SAXOPHONIST MAKES OFF WITH PRICELESS VIOLIN!
    (Krenek, 1927)

K. NAPOLEON WILL LEAVE WIFE FOR SPANISH INFANTA!
    (Kálmán, 1936)

L. 'LARK' FLIES FROM DUTCH VILLAGE TO FIND LOVE!
    (Mascagni, 1917)

M. OPERA SINGER DINES ALONE WITH MOTHER'S PORTRAIT!
    (Herbert, 1914)

N. GYPSY GIRL RESCUED AGAIN BY CATHEDRAL BELL RINGER!
    (Schmidt, 1914)

O. WIVES OUTWIT PHILANDERING HUSBANDS AT FANCY BALL!
    (Heuberger, 1898)

P. LONDON MURDERER JOINS SWEETHEART IN PASSY DREAMS!
    (Taylor, 1931)

Q. GYPSY GIRL RESCUED THIRD TIME BY CATHEDRAL BELL RINGER!
    (Pedrell, 1875)

R. 'SWALLOW' FLIES TO CÔTE D'AZURE TO FIND LOVE!
    (Puccini, 1917)

S. ARTIST'S MODEL SNARES YOUTH FROM PROVENCE!
    (Massenet, 1897)

T. ASSASSINATION ATTEMPT IN PHOTO STUDIO!
    (Weill, 1927)

U. LOUIS V ORDERS ARREST OF HUGUES CAPET!
    (Donizetti, 1832)

V. NOBLEWOMAN POSES AS SHOPGIRL TO SPY ON FIANCÉ!
    (Messager, 1893)

W. NOBLEMAN SMUGGLED PAST SENTRIES IN WATERCART!
    (Cherubini, 1800)

Z. MUSIC-HALL STAR SEDUCES MARRIED MAN!
    (Leoncavallo, 1900)

Pairs

Everybody knows who Papageno and Papagena are, but how about those other pairs – of lovers, parents, gypsies, tramps, and thieves – who appear, usually in supporting roles, in opera? For each of the thirty-five pairs that follow you are asked to name the RELATIONSHIP between the two that make the pair and the OPERA in which they appear. A perfect score is seventy. An opera expert should manage fifty, a fan thirty. As Vortex might have said to Giaour (they're the horses on the ride to Hell in *The Damnation of Faust* and are much too difficult to be in this puzzle), 'Let's get going!'

1. Dancaïre and Remendado

2. Bardolfo and Pistola

3. Sam and Tom

4. Pietro and Paolo

5. Varlaam and Missail

6. Valzacchi and Annina

7. Laca and Števa

8. Clorinda and Tisbe

9. Noémie and Dorothée

10. Tizio and Sempronio

11. Don Federico Herreros and Don Felice de Bornos

12. Nuño and García

13. Gherardo and Nella

14. Talpa and Frugola

15. Billy Jackrabbit and Wowkle

16. Nelusko and Selika

17. Jake and Clara

18. Compère and Commère

19. Peter Quint and Miss Jessel

20. Marco and Giuseppe Palmieri

21. Theodor and Adelaide Waldner

22. Peneios and Gaea

23. Olivier and Flamand

24. Johann and Schmidt

25. Ellen and Rose

26. Sali and Vreli

27. Jack and Bella

28. Mel and Dov

29. Ben and Lucy

30. Poisson and Quinault

31. Nathaniel and Hermann

32. Ighino and Silla

33. Yeroshka and Skula

34. Giannotta and Sandrina

35. Sintolt and Wittig

Sobriquets

'They call me Mimì, but my name is Lucia.' Rodolfo's new sweetheart is hardly the only operatic personage who goes by another name. Here, in rising order of difficulty, are twenty-five pseudonyms, sobriquets, aliases, cognomina, terms of endearment, assumed identities, and assorted monickers, for each of which you are invited to give the true *nom*, *nome*, *Name*, or NAME, and to cite the OPERA in which it appears. (In some cases, the character assumes more than one sobriquet, and occasionally the sobriquet is more familiar than the real name.) A perfect score is fifty. An opera expert should manage forty, a fan twenty-five (this is an easy quiz). As Wolfram said to Tannhäuser (whom he calls Heinrich), 'Vorwärts eilen!'

1. Fidelio

2. Gualtier Maldé

3. Lindoro / Don Alonso

4. Tantris

5. Wehwalt

6. Quinquin / Mariandl

7. Bichette / Resi

8. Idia Legray

9. Manrico

10. Figaro

11. Padre Raffaele / Don Federico Herreros

12. Pereda / Don Felice de Bornos

13. Marquis Renard

14. Mlle Olga

15. Chevalier Chagrin

16. Andrea

17. Ernani

18. Cenerentola

19. Cendrillon

20. Sofronia

21. Timida

22. Mignon

23. Mignon / Eve / Nelli

24. Lulù

25. Jemmy-Legs

Love Is ...

Almost every operatic character feels the pangs of the grand passion, and a few attempt to define or describe it – as bird, boy, sunlight, shadow, fire, water, gift of God, God himself. For each of the following twenty quotations, identify the CHARACTER and the OPERA. A perfect score is forty, but there is a bonus mark somewhere along the way, as one of the quotations comes from a duet where it is sung by two characters (both male). If your score drops below twenty, you may want to re-immerse yourself soon in Wagner's *Liebesnacht*. As Roméo says to Juliette, 'Viens!'

1. 'Love is a rebellious bird that no one can tame. It's useless to call to him if he feels like rejecting you.' (*L'amour est un oiseau rebelle ...*)

2. 'This child, this ivory image of ancient and marvellous craftsmanship – this is Eros. This is love.' (*Cette image d'ivoire, cet enfant ...*)

3. 'Love is the sun of the soul. It is life. Its voice is the beating of our hearts.' (*È il sol dell'anima, la vita è amore ...*)

4. 'Love is the pulsing heartbeat of the universe, of the whole universe – mysterious, sublime, a torment and a delight to the heart.' (*Quell'amor ch'è palpito dell'universo ...*)

5. 'Love, love! You are happiness, torment, sweet intoxication, cruel anxiety. In the pain of you I feel life! One smile from you opens heaven to me!' (*Amore, amore! Gaudio, tormento ...*)

6. 'Love is like the shadow that pursues the one who flees it, and flees the one who pursues it.' (*L'amor ... è come l'ombra ...*)

7. 'Hear me! You do not know what love is. Love is a gift of God. Don't despise it. Love is the life and soul of the world.' (*Udite! Non conoscete amor ...*)

8. 'You who know what love is – you ladies – see if I have it in my heart ... I feel an affection full of desire that now is pleasure and now is pain.' (*Voi che sapete che cosa è amor ...*)

9. 'It's a natural remedy with no after-effects, and no druggist knows how to make it. It's a soothing balm that brings sure relief.' (*È naturale, no da disgusto* ...)

10. 'Love is a little thief, a little snake. He gives the heart peace, and then he takes it away, just as he pleases.' (*È amore un ladroncello, un serpentello* ...)

11. 'This something I cannot name exactly, but I can feel it, here, burning like fire. Can this discovery be love? Yes, yes, it *is* love! It can only be love!' (*Dies Etwas kann ich zwar nicht nennen* ...)

12. 'A miraculous spring appears before me. My soul gazes on it, full of astonishment. From it my soul creates wonders, full of grace. It quickens my heart in ways I cannot name ... You nobles may read from these words what I understand love's purest essence to be.' (*Mir zeiget sich ein Wunderbronnen* ...)

13. 'Lady Love – don't you know her? Don't you know the might of her magic? She is queen over even the proudest hearts. She has power over everything that happens on earth.' (*Frau Minne kenntest du nicht?* ...)

14. 'The highest need of holiest Love, the scorching need of searing Love, burns bright in my breast, drives me to deeds and death.' (*Heiligster Minne höchste Not* ...)

15. 'Perhaps it is the taste of love. They say that love has a bitter taste. But what does it matter?' (*Doch es schmekte vielleicht nach Liebe* ...)

16. 'While Love was with thee, I was present: Love and I are one.'

17. 'Love is a plaintive song sung by a suff'ring maid, telling a tale of wrong, telling of hope betrayed.'

18. 'Oh, Captain Shaw! Type of true love kept under! Could thy Brigade with cold cascade quench my great love, I wonder!'

19. 'Love hears, Love knows, Love answers him across the silent miles, and goes.'

20. 'When genius leaves contemplation for one moment of reality, then Eros is in the word.'

What Opera Are You Watching?

This *Meistersinger* fan occasionally has a midsummer nightmare. He is watching the last scene of his favourite opera, and suddenly he sees Fritz Kothner take young Walther by the shoulder and say, 'Nice try, kid! But I think even you will agree that we have to give the prize to this other fellow, Beckmesser. He's got a great way with a song, and besides, the crowd would have our heads if we judged in favour of anyone else. They love him in this town, you understand. Maybe you can try again next year.'

I've never seen it happen quite that way on the stage, but there are several familiar operatic situations that do, in relatively unfamiliar operas, take surprisingly different turns. In each of the following you are invited to name the COMPOSER and the OPERA in which a familiar action seems at least slightly askew.

A perfect score is fifty. An apprentice opera fan might then consider fifteen a passing mark. A journeyman ought to score twenty, and an opera master more than forty. So 'Fanget an!' What opera are you watching when ...?

1. A beautiful young girl in Nagasaki contracts a temporary marriage with a French naval officer, but he leaves her, dropping lotus blossoms in the sea, and never returns.

2. Marcello sings an aria to the pillow where he says Musetta will never again lay her head.

3. An innocent young man from the provinces secures his family's permission to marry a Parisienne, provided she is virtuous. She isn't; she fills him in on the facts, and leaves him forever.

4. Otello and Desdemona kiss and make up.

5. Falstaff is surprised a second time at Ford's house and escapes disguised as a fat lady.

6. Romeo leads an armed attack on the Capulet palace to rescue Juliet.

7. Rocco gets the gun away from Leonore, who is then imprisoned with her Florestan. Marzelline saves the day by stealing the keys and opening the door.

8. Orpheus is delighted at having lost Eurydice, but is forced by Public Opinion to descend to Hades and rescue her. She in turn is delighted when, with his backward look, he loses her a second time (she finds Jupiter much more attractive).

9. Ariadne frees Mélisande and several other ladies from an underground vault, but the ladies nonetheless opt to return to serve their husband.

10. Barak tries to persuade Calaf not to attempt Turandot's riddles.

11. Salome pleads to save the Baptist's life. When the executioner appears with a dripping sword, she draws a dagger and turns on Herodias. Discovering only then that Herodias is her mother, she plunges the dagger into her own breast.

12. Hansel and Gretel sing a children's prayer while a friend of the family shoots himself.

13. Dimitri rejects Marina for Boris Godunov's daughter Xenia, and is shot and killed by Shuisky.

14. Cherubino, a dashing young officer of seventeen, is in love simultaneously with a countess, a baroness, and an opera star, but finally settles for a childhood sweetheart.

15. Count Almaviva discovers that, while he was away on a diplomatic mission to Mexico, the Countess has had a child by Cherubino.

16. Don Giovanni, disguised as a monk, visits Donna Anna in a cloister, at the monument to her dead husband, the Commendatore.

17. A lecherous adventurer seduces a young girl, whose marble statue confronts him on his wedding night, holds him fast, and drags him off amid flames.

18. Aeneas sails away to found Rome, and Dido's self-immolation is interrupted by her African suitor Iarbas, who persuades her to accept his previously rejected suit.

19. A Druid priestess falls in love with the son of a Roman governor, but kills him in patriotic fury when her people revolt against the occupying forces.

20. Landgraf Hermann brings the four-year-old Elisabeth from Hungary to the Wartburg to marry his son Ludwig.

21. Walter seduces an orphan girl, who is then changed by Alberich into a Rhinemaiden so she can lure Walter to death in the waves.

22. The ruler of the dwarfs cannot live without human love, so he leaves his golden treasure in the earth and visits the upper world, only to be rejected.

23. The Norns and Valkyries get together with assorted nixies and pixies for a *ballet obligatoire*.

24. Wagner leaves Faust's service to become *rector magnificus* of the University of Wittenberg.

25. Hans Sachs enters the singing contest, loses, is run out of Nuremberg – and still gets the girl.

The Eyes Have It

The windows of the soul are often the subjects of song in opera. From Wotan willing his daughter into mortality by kissing her eyes, to the Sandman filling Hansel and Gretel's little peepers, from Desdemona knowing that she will weep because her eyelids burn, to Jenůfa exclaiming that Laca's tormented eyes see right through her – the eyes of opera seem to be everywhere. Here, for a possible fifty points, are twenty-five quotations about eyes, ranged more or less in chronological order. Give yourself one point for each CHARACTER and, somewhat more easily, another point for each OPERA. A clear-sighted opera fan should get thirty-five. Anyone who scores less than fifteen had better get to vision specialist Coppélius soon for a fitting.

1. 'May sweet oblivion lull your fond desires, my child. Rest, thieving eyes! When you are open, you cause mischief enough, and when you are shut, you still do your work.' (*Oblivion soave ...*)

2. 'Open those eyes of yours a little, you foolish, deluded men. Take a good look at women.' (*Aprite un po' quegli occhi ...*)

3. 'I swear it by your eyes, don't be shy! I swear it by our love!' (*Lo giuro agli occhi tuoi ...*)

4. 'Pretty little eyes, don't be shy! Turn those two lovely lamps this way a little.' (*Non siate ritrosi, occhietti vezzosi ...*)

5. 'A holy Will rules in heaven ... His eye, forever pure and clear, keeps all creation in His love.' (*... Das Auge, ewig rein und klar, nimmt aller Wesen liebend wahr.*)

6. 'Does the dwarf know nothing of the golden eye that wakes and sleeps in turn?' (*Nichts weiss der Alp von des Goldes Auge ...*)

7. 'Through a cleft the star of her eye still streams upon me.' (*Des Auges Stern strahlt mich noch an ...*)

8. 'Look me in the eye. Don't try to deceive me.' (*Sieh mir ins Auge ...*)

9. 'Because I am the one who preserved your eye ... I saw what you could not see. I went to him, I looked into his eyes.' (*Weil für dich im Auge das Eine ich hielt ...*)

10. 'With the eye that I have not you are looking at the eye that I have.' (*Mit dem Auge, das als andres mir fehlt ...*)

11. 'He looked up, not at the sword, not at my hand – he looked into my eyes.' (*... Er sah mir in die Augen.*)

12. 'With her eyes ashine, she pointed at what I longed for so – the fruit of the tree of life.' (*Mit Augen winkend ...*)

13. 'And on the boy, with malevolent glance, she cast a bloody, evil eye.' (*... L'occhio affiggeva torvo, sanguigno!*)

14. 'One of them is fat and deaf as a post. The other emaciated, dark, and his eyes – good heavens, what eyes!' (*... Occhi – ciel, quali occhi!*)

15. 'The blind woman has the evil eye.' (*La cieca ha il mal occhio.*)

16. 'Sometimes two thieves – a pair of pretty eyes – steal all the jewels out of my strongbox.' (*... Due ladri, gli occhi belli.*)

17. 'But give her black eyes!' (*Ma falle gli occhi neri.*)

18. 'In the dead of night that child appears to me, covered with blood, eyes on fire, little hands clenched, pleading for mercy.' (*... Óchi, pyláyut, stisnuv ruchónki*)

19. 'Dream, while you're fighting, that a dark eye is watching you, and love awaiting you.' (*Songe en combattant qu'un oeil noir te regarde ...*)

20. 'When I close my eyes, I see a humble cottage, a little house, all white, deep in the woods.' (*En fermant les yeux ...*)

21. 'So long as I see these eyes open, these eyes which are the limits of my vision ... what does sleep matter to me?' (*Pourvu que je voie ces yeux toujours ouverts ...*)

22. 'Weep, my eyes!' (*Pleurez, mes yeux!*)

23. 'They could give God lessons in innocence ... You could say that the angels of heaven are forever performing baptisms there. I know those eyes. I've seen them at work. Shut them!' (*Ils donneraient à Dieu des leçons d'innocence ...*)

24. 'It is his eyes above all that are terrible. They are like black caverns where dragons dwell. They are like black lakes troubled by fantastic moons.' (*Seine Augen sind von allem das Schrecklichste ...*)

25. 'Now he's trying to see which window is mine. Look at his eyes – what big, serious eyes they are!' (*... Schau seine Augen an, was das für grosse ernste Augen sind.*)

The Moon Is Like the Moon

'The moon is like the moon. That is all.' So the common-sense Herodias abruptly calls to a halt the procession of fanciful moon similes made by virtually every character in *Salome*. Here, in rising order of difficulty, are twenty-five other operatic characters observing or commenting on night's luminous orb. For each quotation, you are invited to name the CHARACTER and the OPERA. Out of a possible fifty points, a score of twenty-five merits you a delicious serving of green cheese, while forty qualifies you for the next landing. Anyone who scores a full fifty must be the man in the moon – or is Vera Charles right when she sings, in *Mame*, 'The man in the moon is a lady'?

1. 'Chaste goddess, you ensilver these holy, ancient trees.' (*Casta Diva, che inargenti queste sacre antiche piante* ...)

2. 'Winter storms have waned to the wondrous moon.' (*Winterstürme wichen dem Wonnemond.*)

3. 'We have the moon for our neighbour here.' (*Qui la luna l'abbiamo vicina.*)

4. 'The night was still and lovely, the sky serene, and the moon showed her silver face.' (*Tacea la notte placida* ...)

5. 'Hide yourself, Moon! If you are too embarrassed, then shut your eyes!' (*Mond, verstecke dich dazu* ...)

6. 'There's not a trace upon her face of diffidence or shyness.'

7. 'Fair moon, to thee I sing, bright regent of the heavens.'

8. 'Between sky and sea we shall soon see the moon set.' (*Fra cielo e mar vedrem fra poco tramontar la luna.*)

9. 'A pale ray of eerie moonlight glanced on the fountain. A stifled groan came sounding on the wind.' (*Colpia la fonte un pallido raggio di tetra luna* ...)

10. 'I am like the moon goddess, the little moon goddess who descends by night from the bridge of heaven.' (*Somiglio la Dea della luna* ...)

11. 'O severed head! O bloodless one! How the graveyards are awaiting your deathly light!' (*O testa mozza! O esangue! ...*)

12. 'How red the moon rises!' (*Wie der Mond rot aufgeht!*)

13. 'The moon is white, the cats are crying.' (*Myésats yédet, kotyónok pláchet.*)

14. 'Let us wait till the moon has broken through that great cloud bank.' (*Attendons que la lune ait déchiré ce grand nuage.*)

15. 'On such a night chaste Diana at last let fall her diaphanous veil before Endymion's eyes.' (*Par une telle nuit la pudique Diane ...*)

16. 'Phoebe, I think, casts her inconstant light on false oaths and laughs at lovers.' (*Phoebé, de ses rayons inconstants, j'imagine, éclaire le parjure et se rit des amants.*)

17. 'This lanthorn is the Moon; I, the man i' th' Moon.'

18. 'Today I shall roam as far as the moon-mountains and send my hounds over the dark water.' (*Heute streif' ich bis an die Mondberge ...*)

19. 'O moon, high up in heaven, you travel 'round the world and watch people in their houses.' (*Měsíčku na nebi hlubokém ...*)

20. 'The still moon floods the upper air with a pale ray.' (*La luna immobile innonda l'etere d'un raggio pallido.*)

21. 'The moon is gone. The branch is bare. That's why it's so dark around here.' (*Der Mond ist fort, der Ast ist leer, drum ist's so dunkel ringsumher!*)

22. 'We don't need any light. The moon is shining.' (*Wir brauchen kein Licht, der Mond scheint!*)

23. 'I have made a telescope so powerful that I can see both the surface and the centre of the moon – not just the kingdoms and provinces, but the houses, the squares, and the people.' (*Ho fatto un canocchiale che arriva a penetrar cotanto in dentro ...*)

24. 'First it's up to the moon, then it's down to the cellar – a man could break his legs!' (*Jednou na Měsíc, podruhé do sklepa ...*)

25. 'Look at the moon! How strange the moon seems! She is like a woman rising from a tomb.' (*Sieh die Mondscheibe ...*)

Lim'ricked Librettos

The classic description of the limerick and its limitations runs roughly as follows:

The lim'rick's a joke anatomical
In metrical form economical
    But the good ones I've seen
    Very seldom are clean,
And the clean very seldom are comical.

Now you are invited to prove the untruth of that last line by providing, for each of the ten quatrains below, a reasonably antiseptic LAST LINE of your own – unanatomical, nonetheless comical. And of course you should name the opera you have successfully lim'ricked. Our specimens draw on the time-honoured traditions of masculine/feminine endings, abbreviations to be unabbreviated, and deliberately outlandish translingual equivalents (remember Cole Porter's English rhymes for 'Padua' in *Kiss Me, Kate*). All that may make this lowly art form sound more demanding than it is. Actually, when we asked Rodolfo what he thought of the limerick, he exclaimed, 'La brevità, gran pregio!' And Hans Sachs, while stressing that the limerick was more in Beckmesser's line, agreed to try his hand at our *Gassenhauer*. Both of them scored a perfect ten. *Et vous, Messiers/Dames?* In what opera does it happen that ...?

1. A courtesan nat'rally gifted
    Finds her life, of a sudden, uplifted
        By a young man's affection
        And says in dejection ...

2. In Act 1, by the old riverside,
   A strange sort of boat is espied.
   > In Act 2 a shrew
   > Starts a hullabaloo ...

   _____

3. When he sings 'Donna non vidi mai'
   We think he's a regular gai.
   > Then the girl that he's courted
   > Gets jailed and deported ...

   _____

4. It begins with 'A moi les plaisirs,'
   And the melodies pour out your ears
   > Till you're gloriously soused,
   > It's not Goethe's *Faust* ...

   _____

5. In the shadowy streets of old Mantua,
   If suitably paid in advantua,
   > Your opponent's done in.
   > But you lose your own skin ...

   _____

6. In the forests of far-off Bohemia
   (no trees than Bohemia's are dreamia)
   > Seven bullets are cast.
   > She gets shot with the last ...

   _____

7. Says Urban IV with finality,
   'For your lechery and prodigality
   > You can never be shriven.'
   > Says he, 'Pope, what's livin' ...

   _____

8. They are reading the tale of Sir Lancelot.
   She finds herself looking askance a lot.
      She is killed for a kiss,
      And the moral is this ...

---

9. It's an old and not oft-performed score,
   But it sure leaves you asking for more
      When Paris tells Helen,
      'Now stop all yer yellin' ...

---

10. One conductor said, 'Turn any page an' see –
    What blows out at you is a ragin' sea!'
       Where this guy and his goil
       Get away to would foil ...

Deconstruction in Dixie

To mark the bicentenary of Mozart's birth in 1956, W.H. Auden penned a 'Metalogue to The Magic Flute' in which he mused bemusedly about the liberties upstart directors were taking with traditional operatic staging. He singled out especially

> ... Z the Designer
> Who sets the whole thing on an ocean liner,
> The girls in shorts, the men in yachting caps.

In the years since, with the advent of Deconstructionism, things have got much worse: *Carmen* set in an automobile junkyard, *Figaro* in the Trump Tower, *Aida* in Nazi Germany. The wide-eyed despoilers haven't the decency, when they change everything else, to change the names of the operas they deconstruct. So here are three plot synopses Peter Sellars hasn't thought up yet. You are invited to rename (he won't) the OPERA in question, and allot new monikers to the CHARACTERS therein. The action in each case has been transferred to those storied lands, the southern United States. So take your stand in Dixieland.

A FLORIDA MILLIONAIRE has passed away on his luxurious yacht. His relatives, who hope to invest profitably in a string of luxury hotels on Miami Beach, eagerly hunt down his will and discover that 'our land-o' has been bequeathed by the historically minded patriarch to the old church in St Augustine. Since only the relatives know that the millionaire is dead, one of them, a wide-eyed JUNIOR MAFIOSO from Okefenokee, no slouch himself at fibbing, enlists the services of a deceitful GODFATHER whose PRETTY DAUGHTER he has seen swimming where the boys are. She tells her papa that if she can't have her pining mafioso lover, she'll throw herself overboard into the Swanee River. Devious daddy calls for a notary, gets into the millionaire's deathbed, impersonates his high-pitched squeal, and bequeaths all the millions to himself. The relatives can do nothing, as Florida law has blades ever-ready for those who tampa with wills. They are driven away by the triumphant godfather, who now plans to develop his own Epcot and, with no sense of impending disaster, sends the lovers to honeymoon at the Watergate.

The somewhat fruity OLD FOUNDER of a religious cult in Virginia is shocked to discover that a YOUNG COMPOSER in his fold has been to Alexandria and become infatuated with an EXOTIC DANCER in the Thailand Dance Hall there. The young man, a pure-minded sort *au fond*, dreams that he sees his lady appearing bare-legged in a cheap joint in Bangkok. He sets off for Asia to convert her, but meets first a former SCHOOL CHUM who informs him that the lady is still there in old Virginny, and that he himself is discreetly paying for her services. The innocent boy finds the lady in the lap of luxury and persuades her to change her ways, which she does when she hears his meditative *Mass in A*. He carries her back across the bluegrass mountains till she drops exhausted in a Virginia creepers retreat. Fleeing by helicopter back to his cult founder, the boy, no longer so pure minded, dreams again of his lady of the bare legs, and runs off to her, ready now for a real night in Bangkok. She, never fully recovered from her cross-country, dies singing that the State of Virginia is the only place for her.

A SOUTHPAW KID from the North is trying to crash the starting rotation of the Orioles' pitching staff. His prize pitch, which he seems to lift from his shoestrings, is a soaring riser with lots of zing. But he fails to win the approval of the old-school TEAM MANAGER (nicknamed 'Six Toes' after a lawn-mower accident). The kid cuts quite a cute figure at practice sessions, though, and attracts the attention of the NUBILE DAUGHTER of the team's immensely wealthy OWNER. A friendly BAT BOY and a mature FEMALE REPORTER give the kid a few pointers on how to crash the big leagues, and a trial run impresses the kindly PITCHING COACH, a White Sox veteran. Properly instructed, the young hurler gets his big chance in a Labour Day weekend series at Camden Yards, and he sends the cackling Blue Jays packing with his master zinger. The crowd goes wild and the Baltimore owner is so overwhelmed he bestows on the rookie his only daughter along with – incredible – no salary cap and a share in the team profits.

Hits, Runs, and Errors

Only baseball fans are as avid as opera lovers at toting up the hits, runs, and errors of their favourite performers. Here is a series of operatic clues to the names of twenty-five great and not-so-great baseball stars both past and present, ranged alphabetically by last name from A to Z – but without an entry for X, as the record books show that no player with that final initial ever made it to the big leagues. Each entry provides two operatic clues, one to the gentleman's (sometimes cognominal) FIRST NAME, and one to his (sometimes differently spelled) LAST NAME. Thus if, for the entry under R, the clues were 'Britten loner / Strauss-Hofmannsthal prop,' you ought to answer 'Pete Rose.' For the sports-minded who may not have picked up the *Peter Grimes* and *Der Rosenkavalier* clues, an additional clue about hits, runs, or errors is provided; in the case of Mr Rose it would be a note to the effect that he batted out the most hits (4256) in baseball history. Please note that AL stands for American League, NL for National League, HR for home runs, RBI for runs batted in, and MVP for Most Valuable Player award. Despite any impression conveyed by the foregoing, this is an easy puzzle. So, as they sing at Glimmerglass, 'Play ball!'

A. Lucy's brother / Moses' brother
   (hammerin' Milwaukee-Atlanta outfielder with record 755 HRs)

B. *Carmen* composer / *Lakmé* song
   (tolling Toronto-Chicagoan with record 3 HRs in '88 opening game)

C. Lahore ruler / Donizetti opera
   (indomitable Ebbets Field catcher with record 3 MVPs)

D. Carmen Jones's soldier / Giordano's 'un bel di'
   (joltin' Yankee clipper, connected in 56 consecutive games)

E. Puccini Jackrabbit / the late Sir Geraint
   (eagle-eyed umpire elected to Baseball Hall of Fame in '73)

F. Name for Lulu / mate for Sharpears
   (scrappy Chicago second baseman, AL MVP in '59)

G. Wagner fowler / *Emperor Jones* composer
   (lanky Detroit slugger, hit 58 HRs in '38, even with absences for Jewish holy days)

H. Porgy's Row / Max's profession
   (cunning Oakland hurler, pitched perfect game in '68)

I. Verdi predecessor / critic Kolodin with lost letter
   (quiet Giant from Negro, Cuban, and Mexican leagues, led NL in RBIs in '51)

J. Wagner wooer / Puccini bandit
   (honest Senator and 'fastest pitcher in the history of the game')

K. Wagner king / Marke's title
   (hustling shortstop in World Series as Yank, Cub, Giant)

L. Donizetti heir / Verdi opera
   (schnozzy Boston catcher, led NL at bat in '38 and '42)

M. Glyndebourne impresario / Meyerbeer zealot
   (gentlemanly Giant pitcher, won 373 games in 17 seasons)

N. Falstaff's prince / updated Wagner sinner
   (triumphant Tiger tosser, won 25 games in '45)

O. *Fantasia* mouse / Britten pacifist
   (top-flight Brooklyn catcher, let would-be last ball of '41 World Series game
   slip fatally from his hands)

P. Argento prop / Verdi Windsor wife
   (loose-limbed shut-out ace, moved from Negro to Major Leagues at age 42)

Q. Verdi prince / Britten + Puccini ghosts
   (disabled Red Sox infielder, led International League outfielders in assists in '88)

R. *Jenůfa* victim / Gilbert and Sullivan's 'stupid nurs'ry maid'
   (the Caruso of baseball, 'holder of many home run and other batting records')

S. Wagner lover / Mozart priest
   (speedy Boston-Cleveland outfielder, batted amazing .344 over 22 seasons)

T. Manrico's composer / Manrico's prison (Italian)
   (a Brave like his brother, a champion Yankee manager)

U. Bella's beloved / Met designer
   (right-hander with Kansas City and the Cards, had a 15-15 record)

V. J. Strauss prison warden / unrealized Smetana heroine
   (high-strung Boston southpaw, Cy Young Award winner in '88)

W. Wagner shoemaker / *Meistersinger* composer
   (bow-legged Pirate with eight batting titles, called 'the greatest shortstop in
   baseball history')

Y. Rossini Babylonian / description of Henze Lord
   (cyclonic fastball pitcher with 511 wins in 22 seasons)

Z. Wagner Minnesinger / *Soldaten* composer
   (disingenuous Giant infielder, chased a winning White Sox run home in
   '17 World Series)

I Heard It at the Movies I

Remember the aria from *Aida* in *And the Ship Sails On*? Or the orchestral bit from *Parsifal* in *Kiss of the Spider Woman*? Here are descriptions of twenty-five scenes from movies domestic and foreign, arranged in order of release from Depression years to the present. In every scene an operatic selection figures prominently. You are invited to name the SELECTION and the MOVIE, for a possible fifty points. Even a cinemaphobe operaphile ought to score twenty or more.

A true cinemaddict can extend his/her score to a possible one hundred points by naming in addition the fifty actors who played the CHARACTERS CAPITALIZED in the scene descriptions. If any reader scores a full one hundred, perhaps the Los Angeles–based first editor of *The Opera Quarterly* will see the Academy of Motion Picture Arts and Sciences about a special honorary Oscar.

1. Paris Opéra, sometime in memory. Aspiring American singer PAUL ALLISON, with stolen ticket, watches rapturously as MARCIA MORNAY, American protégée of insanely jealous NICOLAI NAZAROFF, wows 'em in French pants part.

2. Kriegsgefangenen Lager 17, Hallbach, 1914. ROSENTHAL and other prisoners use climactic phrase from French opera (based on German classic) to warn incoming Frenchmen DE BOELDIEU and MARÉCHAL to hide gold watches from German captors.

3. New York. Poor tenement liberally hung with reproductions of Italian Madonnas. Newly shorn JOE BONAPARTE, about to launch middleweight career in ring, plays French opera excerpt on Stradivarius PAPA BONAPARTE bought for twenty-first birthday.

4. Swank government office in mythical kingdom of Tomainia. Diminutive protofascist ADENOID HYNKEL lifts illuminated globe and, easier than Atlas, makes it soar aloft. Surreal effect enhanced by ethereal German prelude on sound track.

5. Well-appointed room in New York. Faltering attempt at Italian aria. Vocal

coach SIGNOR MATISTI, fearful for reputation, assures millionaire CHARLES that wife SUSAN has no future in opera: 'People will think ...' Husband counters, 'I'm something of an authority about what people will think. The newspapers, for example.'

6. Metropolitan Opera House, New York. Baseball-playing priest CHUCK O'MALLEY watches in wings as old flame JENNY LINDEN sways through sultry French opera scene onstage. He leaves early.

7. Metropolitan Opera House, New York. Wine liberally poured out for principals and chorus in Italian opera onstage. Alcoholic DON BIRNAM flees theatre, meets sympathetic HELEN ST JAMES over cloakroom mix-up.

8. Symphony Hall, New York, intercut with stretch of Atlantic seacoast. Brilliant young violinist PAUL BORAY, assisted by massive orchestra and close friend SID JEFFERS at piano, plays own transcription of cosmic-tide German opera as elegantly dressed, nearsighted socialite HELEN WRIGHT drains decanter and staggers across sands to anguished death in towering waves.

9. Death cell in English prison. LOUIS MAZZINI, rightly of aristocratic D'Ascoynes and tenth Duke of Chalfont, remembers how mother eloped with opera-singing father, prompting rejection by family – ALL EIGHT OF WHOM Louis has since killed off or happily seen die.

10. London, Morning room in Algernon Moncrieff's flat in Half-Moon Street. Faltering attempt at Italian aria. Algernon to manservant: 'Did you hear what I was singing, Lane?' Manservant: 'I didn't think it polite to listen, sir.' MR ERNEST WORTHING arrives, reaches for fresh cucumber sandwiches.

11. Teatro Fenice, Venice, 1866. COUNTESS LIVIA SERPIERI in box, LIEUTENANT FRANZ MAHLER among full-dress Austrian soldiers in parterre. Climax of heroic cabaletta. Tricoloured leaflets fall from galleries: 'All foreigners out of Venice.'

12. Living room in Florida bungalow. Polio-stricken MARJORIE LAWRENCE struggles across floor to upset phonograph playing her recording of French opera aria. Husband DR TOM KING comforts her, 'Marge, you've done it ... you've moved!'

13. London bandstand. British intelligence quietly meets Albanian secret agent to arrange for ransom of kidnapped scientist. Band plays Mozart overture. Albanian, skilled in exquisite and efficient torture methods, observes admiringly, 'There's a delicacy and a precision in Mozart's work ...'

14. Demon-haunted castle on lonely Swedish island. Some hour between night and dawn. Birdlike archivist Lindhorst presents for JOHAN and ALMA puppet performance of opera. We perceive that stage hero is not puppet but real man in miniature.

15. Gloomy London flat. Soft-spoken embezzler MARCUS PENDLETON, seated at antique Hopkinson keyboard, discovers that ex–meter maid and secretary PATTY TERWILLIGER, successful at nothing, can manage long-breathed operatic flute solo. Romance blooms.

16. Fairly gloomy London flat, Pembroke Square. Friday. DR DAVID HIRSCH, who shares lover BOB ELKIN with LADY NAMED ALEX, ends long day with patients. Phonograph needle descends to play recording of subtly nuanced operatic trio.

17. Bohemian section of New York. Conscientious cop named FRANK warbles 'Firenze è come un albero fiorito' while driving, then puts another tenor aria on phonograph and carries lunch out into garden. Girl next door asks over fence, 'Is that Björling?' 'No,' he answers, 'it's di Stefano. You can hear it better over here.'

18. Streets of Bloomington, Indiana. Young Italophile cyclist named DAVE warbles German aria in familiar Italian translation while pedalling, under impression that aria, like everything else he loves, is *echt*-Italian.

19. Skies over Vietnam. Megalomaniacal surf-nut LIEUTENANT COLONEL KILGORE leads helicopter raid on defenceless village while tape recorder plays manic Germanic flying music.

20. Briggs Stadium, Detroit, 1949. In open-air ring, JAKE LA MOTTA wrests middleweight crown from Marcel Cerdan. Brutal realism, surreal montage, and slow-motion effects enchanced by ethereal Italian intermezzo on sound track.

21. Rocky pensinsula in northwestern Turkey, 1915. Before senseless battle in which buddies Archie and FRANK will face almost certain death, Major Barton plays male-bonding French opera duet on portable phonograph in trench.

22. Théâtre de les Bouffes du Nord, Paris. Messenger boy Jules surreptitiously captures on high-quality tape recorder elusive voice of silver-gowned black American diva CYNTHIA HAWKINS in far-wandering Italian aria.

23. Countryside beyond San Martino, Tuscany, 10 August 1944. Night of Saint Lawrence, when you wish upon a star. Liberating American army expected any moment. Retreating German soldier sings star-wishing aria in dazed despair.

24. New York. *Times* reporter SYDNEY SCHANBERG wonders if friend DITH PRAN is still alive and in hiding. Italian tenor sings on stereo, 'My secret is locked within me. No one shall know my name.' President on television announces, 'Cambodia is the Nixon doctrine in its purest form.' Tenor sings, 'I shall conquer, I shall conquer.'

25. Rented hall in Brooklyn. Climax of atrociously sung Italian aria. Gasoline-fed fire explodes, sending elegantly groomed MAEROSE and rest of DON CORRADO'S clan scurrying to relative safety of limousines.

I Heard It at the Movies II

Remember Audrey Hepburn playing 'Voi che sapete' on the piano with her father before she left for the convent in *The Nun's Story*? Remember the ominous recurrence of Alvaro's theme from *La Forza del Destino* on the sound track of *Jean de Florette*?

Here are descriptions of twenty-five more scenes from movies domestic and foreign, arranged in order of release from Depression years to the present. In every scene an operatic selection figures prominently. You are invited to name the SELECTION and the MOVIE, for a total of fifty points. An operaphile ought to score twenty or more. A cinemaddict can extend his/her score to a possible one hundred points by naming in addition the fifty actors who played the CHARACTERS CAPI-TALIZED in the scene descriptions. No opera is featured more than once. (It wouldn't do to have twenty of our twenty-five movies feature *Madama Butterfly*!) Tickets, please!

1. New York Opera House. Suspiciously ungirlish gypsy girls on stage turn out to be ne'er-do-wells FIORELLO and TOMASSO. Gypsy hag finishes Italian aria. Mustach-ioed OTIS B. DRIFTWOOD, in box, asks, 'What was that? High C or Vitamin D?'

2. Opera box, St Petersburg. ANNA and VRONSKY, living in sin, watch peasant dance in first scene of Russian opera, awaiting inevitable off-stage scene at inter-mission.

3. Southern France. Fledgling coloratura ANNETTE MONARD, throat festooned with outsize bow, warbles Italian opera aria in music lesson with Uncle Tito, who threatens convent if she won't keep practising. She slips over wall, lands on impecunious American opera composer JONATHAN STREET. Romance blooms.

4. San Marco Opera House, Los Angeles. Epigrammatically wise ORIENTAL DE-TECTIVE politely arranges for madhouse escapee GRAVELLE GRAVELLE to reprise Mephistophelean baritone solo so as to catch real perpetrator of onstage crime.

5. Tivoli Opera House, San Francisco, 1906. Debuting soprano MARY BLAKE wows 'three thousand mugs,' including two-fisted but sensitive FR TIM MULLEN, in

heaven-storming French opera finale. Two-fisted but insensitive BLACKIE NORTON, impressed, says, 'I never caught this opera racket until now. How long has it been going on?'

6. Manhattan Concert Hall, 1937. Teenage PATRICIA CARDWELL, suddenly responsible for one hundred unemployed musicians, sneaks into rehearsal despite tell-tale feather on beanie, and sinks into seat entranced as SILVER-MANED CONDUCTOR conducts German opera prelude without benefit of baton.

7. Opera House, New Orleans, 1841 ('exactly a century ago this coming Saturday'). COUNTESS who is 'not really a countess' stages fainting spell during first-act love duet of *bel canto* Italian opera, attracting attention of singers, conductor, orchestra, gallery, and pompous patron in next box.

8. Paris Opéra, soon to be haunted by mysterious PHANTOM. Leading baritone ANATOLE GARRON, in love with aspiring soprano CHRISTINE DUBOIS, raises curtain with French rendition of German opera drinking song.

9. Elegant cafe in Berlin, 1902. CLIVE CANDY, VC-bedecked hero on leave from Boer War, accompanies very feminine feminist EDITH HUNTER to balcony table with express purpose of provoking reaction over allegations of British atrocities in German newspapers. At his request, band plays French opera aria based on German classic. He provokes entire German army, fights duel with officer THEO KRETSCHMAR-SCHULDORFF.

10. Elegant Victorian home, London. Cryptic verse from Omar's *Rubaiyat* prominently displayed on salon table. LORD HARRY WOTTON says to WAXEN-FACED YOUNG MAN who has just seduced the innocent SIBYL VANE, 'My sister's box number is 27. It's on the grand tier. You'll see her name on the door. I hope to see you before half-past nine. I don't want you to miss de Reszke in the duet,' and exits singing strain from famous Mozart seduction scene.

11. Metropolitan Opera, New York, 1903. Under conductor CARLO SANTI, nervous ENRICO CARUSO, in poorly received debut, sings Italian duet with soprano LOUISE HEGGAR, while wealthy patron Park Benjamin sits stonily in box with already infatuated daughter DOROTHY.

12. Staatsoper, East Berlin, post-war, pre-wall. Onstage SOPRANO launches into final scene from decadent German opera. Cue for black marketeer IVO KERN and kidnapped Englishwoman SUSANNE MALLESON to leave box for sinister streets in attempt to escape to Western sector.

13. Men's washroom at spa hotel near Rome. Factotum movie director GUIDO fears oncoming nervous breakdown as Italian opera overture creeps up on sound track, inviting escape into memories and fantasies.

14. Madrid street. Two-faced (or identical twin) Conchita leaves endlessly frustrated lover gazing at Norn-like woman sewing in shop window. Loudspeakers report political uprisings and violent deaths of prominent clerics, then play politicized German opera duet for twins. Terrorists' bomb explodes in swirl of flames.

15. American ocean resort. LOU watches in apartment across way as lovely clam-bar waitress SALLY switches on cassette of Italian *bel canto* aria and washes away day's labours with freshly cut lemons.

16. Ornate opera house on Amazon. BRIAN SWEENY FITZGERALD and mistress MOLLY arrive late, having rowed downstream for two days and two nights for unique performance of Italian opera with Enrico Caruso and Sarah Bernhardt. Caruso points to Fitzgerald in audience; Fitzgerald takes this as sign.

17. Ancestral home in Sicily. Luigi Pirandello opens window. Mother's ghost appears to tell story of lost innocence, underscored by subtly introduced Mozart aria about losing pin.

18. Poppy field overlooking Florence. Ever-unsatisfied George Emerson kisses proper Edwardian Lucy Honeychurch. On soundtrack, honeyed Italian aria tells how young girl awakes to love with student's kiss.

19. Loft apartment in New York. Career woman ALEX FORREST, in rendezvous with married corporate lawyer DAN GALLAGHER, turns up volume on taped performance of knife-wielding Italian opera death scene. 'It's my favourite opera,' she confides. 'Mine too,' he adds. 'My father took me to the old Met. I was five years old.' Later she wields kitchen knife.

20. Lower-class street in Blitz-weary London. Blimp slips cable and floats skittishly across rooftops to amusement of townsfolk. Sound track plays skittish dance from patriotic German opera.

21. Metropolitan Opera House, Lincoln Center, New York. Moon is full. Love-crazed RONNY CAMMARERI takes vivacious LORETTA CASTORINI to see Italian opera with big moon unauthentically dominating Zeffirelli-style stage set. Moon also affects Loretta's mother (ROSE), father (COSMO), and GRANDFATHER's baying dogs.

22. Dublin. New Year's party at house of Gabriel Conroy's old maiden aunts. Before snow falls, Aunt Julia gives touching rendition of 'Arrayed for the Bridal,' derived from virginal Italian *bel canto* aria.

23. Suburban Atlanta, 1949. Magnolias in bloom. Radio plays Czech opera aria in which lonely spirit longs for human love. DAISY WERTHAN does first nice thing for HOKE COLBURN, hired by son BOOLIE to be her chauffeur.

24. War Memorial Opera House, San Francisco. Billionaire prince charming EDWARD LEWIS and Cinderella streetwalker VIVIEN WARD wing in from Beverly Hills to see Italian opera about courtesan who almost made it to respectability. He issues quiet challenge: those who only appreciate opera, and do not love it, find 'it will never become part of their soul.'

25. Teatro Massimo, Palermo. MICHAEL and KAY, parents of debuting tenorino, watch from box as chorus sings of Resurrection and powerful figures die violently in both Sicily and Rome.

I Heard It at the Movies III

Remember Nelson Eddy as 'the whale who wanted to sing at the Met,' carolling the quintet from *Martha* in a hundred celestial voices in the 1946 Walt Disney cartoon feature *Make Mine Music?* Remember Secret Agent 007 watching the finale of the first act of *Figaro* with a cello-playing Bratislava sniperess in1987's *The Living Daylights?*

Here are the usual police-report descriptions of twenty-five more scenes from movies domestic and foreign, arranged in order of release, from Depression years to the present. In every scene an operatic selection figures prominently. You are invited to name the SELECTION and the MOVIE, for a possible total of fifty points. Even a movie-hating opera fan ought to score twenty points or more. A movie-lover can extend his or her score to a possible one hundred points by also naming the fifty performers who played the CHARACTERS CAPITALIZED in the scene descriptions. No opera is featured more than once. *Allor,* lights! Camera! Action!

1. Country road in U.S., 1935. Probably Saturday afternoon. Devilishly handsome fisherman TOMMY RENWICK offers to fix stranded ANN MERRILL's automobile while car radio plays French opera finale. Tommy sings along with broadcast and tells Ann he's a Metropolitan Opera star, which is not quite true.

2. Lighthouse in U.S., 1936. LIGHTHOUSE KEEPER and his tiny 'daughter' STAR (whose mother was a *bel canto* soprano) join with friendly CAPTAIN to turn Italian opera sextet into improvised trio.

3. Royal Theatre, Montreal, 1930s. Canadian soprano MARIE DE FLOR, performing in castle-top Italian opera finale, keeps imagining she hears love call of distant SERGEANT BRUCE.

4. Theater an der Wien (alias K.K. Priv Theater), Vienna, 5 April 1874. POLDI VOGELHUBER, pathetically faithful wife of great waltz composer 'SHANNI,' rushes frantically to sold-out premiere of his new operetta, featuring rival CARLA DONNER, and halts at top of main aisle as Duvivier camera does fancy work.

5. Cartoon palace of operatic Venetian, imaginary times. Assorted ostriches, hippopotamuses, elephants, and alligators, introduced by witty forties DEAN OF MUSIC, cavort in Italian opera ballet conducted by photogenic forties MAESTRO.

6. Chicago Municipal Opera House, 1930s. Curtain falls on disastrous debut of SUSAN ALEXANDER in new American opera. Newspaper magnate husband CHARLES, fostering her career, glowers in opera box while bored collaborator JEDEDIAH LELAND reduces his program to shreds.

7. Ancona, 1930s. Signor Bragana, proprietor of roadside *ristorante*, gets ovation for badly sung Italian baritone aria in amateur concert as wife Giovanna and handsome drifter Gino begin to think about murdering him.

8. Smart New York apartment with wallpaper miniatures depicting picnicking Wagner family, 1943. Soprano GENYA SMETANA leads uninvited guests in horrendous rendition of German opera chorus. On wall, scores of tiny Wagners, Cosimas, children, dogs, and horses cover ears, pack up, and flee.

9. Concert Hall, New Orleans, 1944. Orchestra finishes transcendent German opera finale. Absorbed ABIGAIL MARTIN brushes against self-absorbed ROBERT MANETTE as she leaves. 'I feel I've lost myself for a long time,' he apologizes. 'When I hear music,' she counters, 'I feel as if something has been added to my life that wasn't there before.'

10. New York recording studio, turn of the century. Portly tenor RICHARD OLSTROM, friend of TWO SISTERS from out of town, records German opera aria under primitive conditions. At playback, faithful dog Tristan perches at gramophone horn, recognizing his master's voice.

11. Parisian house with passe-partout mirrors, 1949. Eurydice cannot understand husband ORPHÉE's fascination with motorcycle-escorted DEATH. Sound track plays otherworldly French opera flute solo.

12. Grand Opera House, 1920s. FEODOR CHALIAPIN, pursued by impresario SOL HUROK, knocks 'em dead in Russian opera of all operas.

13. Savoy Theatre, London 1924. Future Olympic winner HAROLD ABRAHAMS watches rapturously as SIBYL GORDON performs in English operetta trio. 'Isn't she a peach?' exclaims fellow track contender in box. 'She's magnificent!' says Harold. He bravoes. She spots him from the stage and nods. Love blooms.

14. Metropolitan Opera House, New York, 1982. Famous tenor Signore FINI finishes trademark Italian opera aria successfully while fire-breathing dragon, an overactor at rehearsal, behaves himself.

15. Mare Tireno, July 1914. Luxury liner *Gloria N.*, crowded with impossibly vain

opera singers, sights looming island of Erimo, native land of newly deceased soprano Edmea Tetua, whose ashes are scattered as phonograph plays her recording of nostalgic Italian opera aria.

16. Freihaustheater, Vienna, 1791. AUSTRIAN COMPOSER collapses at harpsichord as LIBRETTIST performs folksy glockenspiel aria on stage and implacable RIVAL watches from curtained box.

17. Prison in unspecified Latin American country, 1985. Gay inmate LUIS MOLINA tells straight cellmate and political activist VALENTIN of Nazi propaganda movie in which heroine LENI meets Nazi officer at opulent apartment as magic music from German opera rises on sound track. 'The music is magical,' she says. 'I feel like I'm floating on air.'

18. Atlantic City, 1986. FAST EDDIE FELSON, erstwhile Chicago pool hustler, returns from twenty-five-year exile to help promising young hustler VINCENT and gets fitted for precision glasses to triumphant burst of Italian opera chorus of exiles on sound track.

19. New York, 1986. Opera-loving architect DAVID takes Hannah's sister HOLLY and colleague APRIL on taxi tour of Manhattan's magnificently durable living places. Sound track plays opening measures of Italian opera describing conveniently makeshift housing.

20. Chicago Opera box, 1930. AL CAPONE, weeping through lachrymose Italian opera aria, is told by Frank Nitti that veteran policeman JIM MALONE has just been polished off. Capone smiles sadistically through his tears.

21. San Francisco recording studio, 1993. DANIEL HILLARD, versatile but in-the-doghouse actor soon to pose as English nanny-factotum in order to see his children, dubs Italian opera patter song for cartoon parrot named Pudgy.

22. Philadelphia apartment, 1993. Ambulance-chasing lawyer JOE MILLER hears AIDS victim ANDREW BECKETT explain, via recording of death-haunted Italian opera aria, why operatic singing is important to him.

23. Massively gloomy New England prison, some years back. Lifer ANDY DUFRESNE sends letter duet from Mozart opera out over loudspeaker system. In courtyard with fellow inmates, prison 'fixer' RED wonders what the 'two Italian ladies' are singing about.

24. Elegant house in provincial French town, 1996. Lelièvre family watches Mozart baritone sing serenade in televised opera. Inscrutable MAID and unhinged POST-MISTRESS, having dispatched M. Lelièvre, shoot MME LELIEVE and her children in cold blood.

25. Moby's Winebar, Australian city, 1980s. Dysfunctional adult prodigy DAVID HELFGOTT wows customers with piano solo version of Russian opera instrumental flight of hero transmogrified by swan maiden for eventual reconciliation with oppressive father.

ACT II

Anagrams

Donna Anagram

Twenty-six operatic CHARACTERS, from A to Z, are described below in sentences that suit them to a 'T' and also contain their names in anagrams and/or puns. For example, in the sentence 'These days she might have gone dieseling with her brother through the forest' the answer is Sieglinde – an anagram of 'dieseling.' If you can similarly identify all twenty-six characters you deserve a trip by train or plane to the *opera* house that suited *Milton* Cross to a T. Shall we be off to the *Metropolitan*?

A _ _ _ _ _ _ _   'You tote that bale and I get rich,' said the old man of the river.

B _ _ _ _ _ _ _   He's never drab in Shakespearean phol-de-rol.

C _ _ _ _ _ _ _ _   ''E could give a cop the slip, I tells you,' the inventor complained.

D _ _ _ _ _ _   Do nod off till the cock crows, your majesty.

E _ _ _ _   Oh, this sailor lad is no Peter Grimez.

   _ _ _ _ _ _ _

F _ _ _ _ _ _   He'll give you L if you call him Fatso.

G _ _ _ _ _ _   Did he grunt? Take the wag out of the Wagner thug.

H _ _ _ _ _ _ _   'Call that a hero?' she said. 'I prefer shad roe.'

I _ _ _ _ _ _   Odile's got nothing on this olde gal.

J _ _ _ _ _ _ _   'Will the captain let you and I take his jet?' she asked, ungrammatically.

K _ _ _ _ _   Never mind your parkas. He'll start a spark in the glen.

L _ _ _ _ _ _   ''E certainly alert,' said the grave digger.

M _ _ _ _ _ _ _   Egg this curate on in scrambled omelet.

N _ _ _ _   A Roman was her undoing.

O _ _ _ _ _ _   'I'm a polyphonist,' she sang. (She ought to have been more amply oiled.)

P _ _ _ _ _ _ _   Put in reverse he just about falls apart.

Q _ _ _ _ _ _ _ _ _   'I'm double-O on the Notre Dame squad,' he bellowed, after a fashion.

R _ _ _ _ _ _ _ _   'Either we're outlaws or dead men,' he reminded.

S _ _ _ _ _ _ _   He wouldn't let a spot escape his notice.

T _ _ _ _ _ _ _ _ _ _   'Are you unclean?' the Pope asked him. 'Take a sauna, then!'

U _ _ _ _ _   She could be disarranged by curial investigation.

V _ _ _ _   When under par, she turns to social upstarts like T, above.

W _ _ _ _ _ _ _   'Who won the Rhine River Glide?' she wondered.

X _ _ _ _ _   He's a tree-loving rex in a farce about sex.

Y _ _ _ _ _   He's a mere child in a golden oldy.

Z _ _ _ _ _   Does she realize how close she came? To the nth degree.

Fan Anagrams

So you never heard of Gerda Lammers? Avid fans of hers would say, 'Anyone who didn't like her Elektra should be slung in the slammer.' Similarly, fans of Antonio Scotti will remember, 'His Michonnet was stoic to a T.' If you have a taste for anagram, you are hereby invited to arrange the letters of certain words in each of the comments ranged below – comments that might be made by avid fans – so as to identify twenty-five SINGERS anagrammatically. Each singer is listed by surname, one for each alphabet letter (and we're sorry that once again we couldn't come up with an X). So, as tenors will sometimes say when faced with a high-C aria, 'Transpose!'

A _ _ _ _   They loved his Almaviva even in the Transvaal.

B _ _ _ _ _   She ought to make a stab at la Tosca.

C _ _ _ _ _   She sure gave them L at the Scala.

D _ _ _ _ _ _   He sang all repertories, dooming potential rivals.

E _ _ _ _ _   Her Butterfly could wring tears from a stone.

F _ _ _ _ _ _ _   Her Sieglinde fast made Met audiences glad they came.

G _ _ _ _   His Falstaff was big box office.

H _ _ _ _   He made Met performances shine for – it seems like – fifty-seven years.

I _ _ _ _ _   Her Constanze left audiences all but vowing to return.

J _ _ _ _ _ _   He could outsing ten with his 'Jour est levé.'

K _ _ _   Her Wagner career took off like a Nike.

L _ _ _   Her Lulu was a real lollapalooza.

M _ _ _ _   No one ever put the blame on this dame.

N _ _ _ _ _ _   In candor I must say her Elsa was something else.

O _ _ _ _ _ _ _   Her Fedora was the oil of Gilead poured over your head.

P _ _ _ _ _ _   His Radamès charmed every Nile reptile.

Q _ _ _ _ _ _   His Rigoletto was an unsprung coil on the *qui vive*.

R _ _ _ _   Her arias drove Chicago wild.

S _ _ _ _ _ _   Even the Saints loved her devilish Carmen.

T _ _ _ _ _ _   Long Island heard her Met broadcasts with bated breath.

U _ _ _ _ _ _ _ _   R. Strauss might almost have had a clause in her contract.

V _ _ _ _ _   Her Senta deserved a R(oyal) Navy salvo.

W _ _ _ _ _ _ _ _ _   He almost kept a swan in his dressing room.

Y _ _ _   Rio said 'Oh, yes' to her Isolde.

Z _ _ _ _ _ _ _ _   His Otello held London mostly in amaze.

Academic Patter

If you can see how, to use an earlier example, Sieglinde might have gone dieseling with her brother through the forest, you are invited, from the anagrammatical clues or puns in the right-hand column below, to fill in the NAMES of the appropriate operatic personages or personalities in the blanks provided on the left. Read vertically, the initial letters of your answers will spell out the English TITLE of an unjustly neglected German OPERA. Helpful hint: the opera's composer was christened in honour of the saint who guards the gates of heaven, and rightly so, for you'll find his surname anagrammatically in the first nine letters of the hymn line *in seculorum secula*.

_ _ _ _ _ _   He almost let the ritual die out.

_ _ _ _ _ _   Her husband knows she wears one, but will he tell?

_ _ _ _ _   He's a Puccini hero *en garde*.

_ _ _ _ _ _ _   She's a Fedora for Figaro and Abul Hassan.

_ _ _ _   As an *Akademiker* his patter could make Figaro blush.

_ _ _ _ _ _   In an earlier age his conducting might have been reviewed in the *The Tatler*.

_ _ _ _ _ _ _ _   Glass raised by composer Marc during an air raid

_ _ _ _ _ _   Glass ordered in Spanish by Bellini Villager

_ _ _ _ _   Louis B. would have made this Sam a movie star.

_ _ _ _ _   Cora's crazy to give this Verdi page a movie award.

_ _ _ _ _ _   The wide-ruling Wagner goddess who practically spans a continent

— — — — — — — — —   The Maria sent by fame out of the barrio

— — — — — — — —   Verdi patriarch combining features of both Moses and Aaron

— — — — — — —   Verdi comprimario on stage for two Parisian parties

— — — — — — — — — —   Offenbach villain dressed up before everything Italian

— — — — — — — —   'Hold the fort,' he told his knights, 'as I am doing.'

— — — — — — — — —   'Who,' say fans of his *Pelléas* recording, 'could desire more?'

ACT III

Vertical Patterns

Vertical Patterns I

With this diagram as a guide:

D	I	P	R	O	V	E	N	Z	A	I	L	M	A	R
D	O	N	N	A	N	O	N	V	I	D	I	M	A	I
C	O	N	N	A	I	S	T	U	L	E	P	A	Y	S

use the FAMOUS (stage or recorded) PERFORMANCES clues to write the titles of the appropriate arias, duets, ensembles, etc. in the GRID. Each title is seventeen letters in length. Vertical repetition of the same letter within the boldfaced oblongs will enable you to work upwards and downwards from the starting point you choose. As the three Norns say, beginning their vertical descent, 'Hinab! hinab!'

NOTE: One of the famous performances ended tragically: the name of the artist on that occasion will be spelled out vertically in the thirteen shaded squares. To the memory of that great artist this puzzle is humbly dedicated.

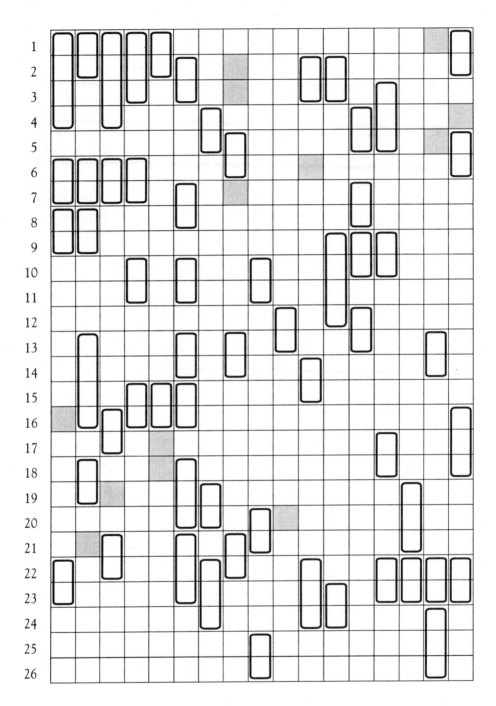

FAMOUS PERFORMANCES

1. Vickers exclaims that Price is too young to die. (Verdi)

2. Warren, after farewell to Tucker, wonders at the mystery of death. (Verdi)

3. Schwarzkopf, confused, thinks Flagstad is in love with her. (Beethoven)

4. Steber remains resolute in face of tortures. (Mozart)

5. Peters taunts eavesdropping new husband Tozzi. (Mozart)

6. Della Casa cautions Gueden to keep clear of Siepi. (Mozart)

7. Gedda prays to forget temptress Sills. (Massenet)

8. Pinza mourns death of Rethberg's mother. (Verdi)

9. Fidès-Devriès savours sweetness of Jean de Reszke. (Massenet)

10. Caruso asks Scotti to swear to dying behest. (Verdi)

11. Matthews sees seraphic vision. (Thomson)

12. Gigli sings of his sweet Homeric passion. (Gluck)

13. Milnes reproaches himself for denouncing Domingo. (Giordano)

14. Ludwig prays to forget tempter Corelli. (Bellini)

15. Fischer-Dieskau opens his wallet to Berry. (Strauss)

16. Schumann-Heink tells lover-to-be Schorr how she likes breakfast eggs. (Wagner)

17. Callas, maddened, remembers di Stefano's beautiful voice. (Bellini)

18. Milanov sends rosy love aloft to imprisoned Björling. (Verdi)

19. Nilsson asks of Hotter a father's pardon. (Wagner)

20. Bergonzi waxes ecstatic when Rysanek says she loves him. (Verdi)

21. Pavarotti recalls droplet forming on Sutherland's eyelash. (Donizetti)

22. Bumbry (or Verrett) hymns Sapphic muse. (Gounod)

23. Pons waltzes blithely after swallow. (Gounod)

24. Tibbett proclaims joys of simple life. (Gershwin)

25. Peerce laughs at death, then clasps Merrill's hand. (Verdi)

26. Bori and Crooks look forward to life in the big city. (Massenet)

Vertical Patterns II

With this diagram as a guide:

D	I	P	R	O	V	E	N	Z	A	I	L	M	A	R
D	O	N	N	A	N	O	N	V	I	D	I	M	A	I
C	O	N	N	A	I	S	T	U	L	E	P	A	Y	S

use the FAMOUS (stage or recorded) PERFORMANCES clues to write the titles of the appropriate arias, duets, ensembles, etc. in the GRID. Each title is sixteen letters in length. Vertical repetition of the same letter within the boldfaced oblongs will enable you to work upward and downward from the starting point you choose. As Hotter, beginning his vertical descent, says to Suthaus, 'Fahren wir nieder.'

NOTE: The name of the artist to whom this puzzle is dedicated will be spelled out vertically in the eleven shaded squares.

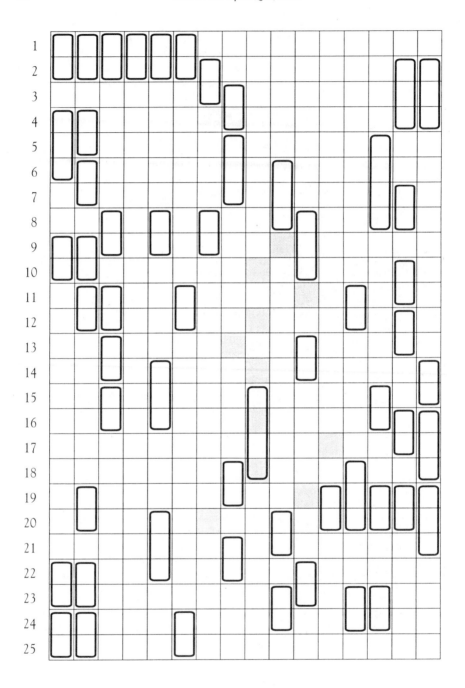

FAMOUS PERFORMANCES

1. Cotrubas, taken captive, asks only to cry. (Handel)

2. Pinza, abandoned, asks only to die. (Monteverdi)

3. Horne, overworked, remembers a tale of long ago. (Rossini)

4. Several Savoyards muse on a peculiar situation. (Sullivan)

5. Stignani asks the Virgin to aid her escape. (Ponchielli)

6. Schumann tells Melchior and Schorr of her happiness. (Wagner)

7. Callas pleads with Ludwig to care for her children. (Bellini)

8. Windgassen, kissed by Mödl, remembers another's pain. (Wagner)

9. Crooks tells how he closed his eyes and dreamed. (Massenet)

10. Supervia reads her death in the cards. (Bizet)

11. Merrill, facing death, tells Stevens she will be proud of him. (Bizet)

12. D'Oyly Carte chorus prepares for battle. (Sullivan)

13. Glyndebourne ensemble declares Lewis a patriot. (Sullivan)

14. Singher apostrophizes his magic ring. (Offenbach)

15. Leontyne Price anticipates her second wedding night. (Strauss)

16. Gobbi approaches an ominous oak tree. (Verdi)

17. Caruso sees colour contrasts between mistress and model. (Puccini)

18. Stratas wishes she were a lady, not a lady's maid. (Mozart)

19. Met chorus returns home from battle. (Gounod)

20. Pavarotti remembers wonderful nights with Freni. (Puccini)

21. Domingo asks Te Kanawa about his mother. (Bizet)

22. Sutherland anticipates her first wedding night. (Bellini)

23. Schipa reproaches Poli for having betrayed him. (Donizetti)

24. Seefried looks forward to winning Fischer-Dieskau's favour. (Handel)

25. Albanese is startled by the sudden appearance of her son. (Puccini)

Vertical Patterns III

With this diagram as a guide:

M	O	R	I	R	S	I	P	U	R	A	E	B	E	L	L	A
M	O	R	I	R	T	R	E	M	E	N	D	A	C	O	S	A
M	I	R	I	S	T	S	O	W	U	N	D	E	R	B	A	R

use the FAMOUS (stage or recorded) PERFORMANCES clues to write the titles of
the appropriate arias, duets, ensembles, etc. in the GRID. Each title is fifteen letters
in length. Vertical repetition of the same letter within the boldfaced oblongs will
enable you to work upwards and downwards from the starting point you choose. As
you move vertically, resolve, with Gluck's Orpheus descending, 'tutti quei superar!'

NOTE: The name of the artist to whose memory this puzzle is dedicated will be
spelled out vertically in the nine shaded squares.

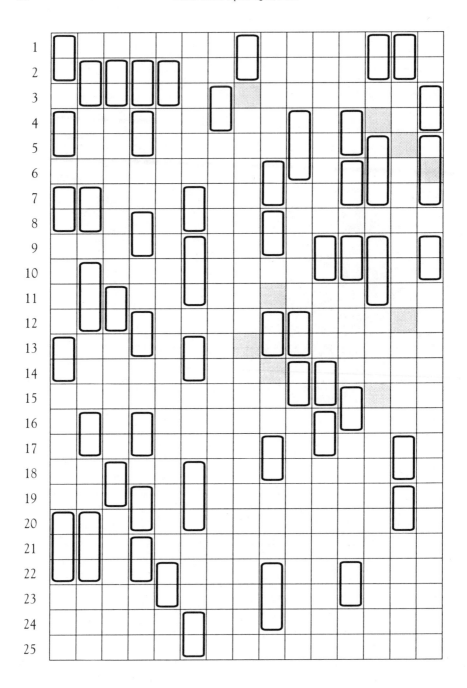

FAMOUS PERFORMANCES

1. Merrill urges Bergonzi to come home to Provence. (Verdi)

2. Björling exclaims over Albanese's beauty. (Puccini)

3. Stevens asks Crooks if he knows a land of orange trees. (Thomas)

4. Vezzani tells Journet he wants pleasure above all. (Gounod)

5. Callas, dying, says goodbye to past happiness. (Verdi)

6. Christoff laments that Stella never loved him. (Verdi)

7. Pinza invites Rethberg to his castle. (Mozart)

8. Hampson proclaims his more-than-tonsorial skills. (Rossini)

9. Carreras touches Stratas's cold little hand. (Puccini)

10. Peerce tells Berger that love is the sun of the soul. (Verdi)

11. Galli-Curci gives de Luca a message for his daughter. (Verdi)

12. Price hopes that Domingo will return victorious. (Verdi)

13. Tebaldi pleads with daddy Corena. (Puccini)

14. Von Stade surrenders to Hadley's pretending. (Kern)

15. Battistini hopes to add ten more names to his list. (Mozart)

16. Garden lets her hair down and sings a litany. (Debussy)

17. Jurinac finds a new father in an enemy land. (Mozart)

18. Dermota invites Gueden to drink and forget. (J. Strauss)

19. Anderson wonders if jewels can compensate for lost honour. (Bernstein)

20. Vickers comes madly out of the storm. (Britten)

21. Novotná tells Sayão what it's like to be in love. (Mozart)

22. Prey insists that he and Schreier are perfect male specimens. (Mozart)

23. Thill vainly regrets he must leave Carthage. (Berlioz)

24. Welitsch hears strains of her homeland. (J. Strauss)

25. McCormack exclaims at Bori's moonlit beauty. (Puccini)

Vertical Patterns IV

With this diagram as a guide:

D	I	P	R	O	V	E	N	Z	A	I	L	M	A	R
D	O	N	N	A	N	O	N	V	I	D	I	M	A	I
C	O	N	N	A	I	S	T	U	L	E	P	A	Y	S

use the FAMOUS (stage or recorded) PERFORMANCES clues to write the titles of the appropriate arias, duets, ensembles, etc. in the GRID. Each title is thirteen letters in length. Vertical repetition of a letter within the boldfaced oblongs will enable you to work upward and downward from the starting point you choose. Mozart's *Idomeneo* figures heavily in this puzzle, so 'Sù, sù! partiamo or' or.'

NOTE: This quiz is fondly dedicated to the founding editor of *The Opera Quarterly*, whose name will be spelled out vertically in the ten shaded squares.

FAMOUS PERFORMANCES

1. Schwarzkopf releases Ludwig to wed Stich-Randall. (R. Strauss)

2. Domingo agrees that it is best not to dwell on misfortune. (Puccini)

3. Patzak dallies with Gueden, unaware that she is his wife. (J. Strauss)

4. Mödl tells Windgassen that she knew him when he was a baby. (Wagner)

5. Thebom warns Flagstad and Suthaus that the night will soon end. (Wagner)

6. Lehmann tells Melchior that he is spring after winter. (Wagner)

7. Masterson, Wright, and Reed find themselves in a dilemma. (Sullivan)

8. Drummond-Grant flatters Watson to get the tower keys. (Sullivan)

9. Savoyard cast sing that the lovers will be parted by a dungeon cell. (Sullivan)

10. Van Dam regrets having raised a sword against Behrens. (R. Strauss)

11. Nilsson goes mad, tormented by the Furies. (Mozart)

12. Berger tells Lemnitz that hell's fury burns in her heart. (Mozart)

13. Cretan chorus exclaims over the vow that Pavarotti has taken. (Mozart)

14. Farrell keens at her husband's funeral. (Gershwin)

15. Norman foresees the fall of king and city. (Berlioz)

16. Varnay tries to lure Vinay to further dalliance. (Wagner)

17. Caruso dons a clown's smock and greasepaint. (Leoncavallo)

18. Simoneau sings of the sweetness of love's aura. (Mozart)

19. Warren invites a Cypriot chorus to wet their whistles. (Verdi)

20. Capsir hears Borgioli's voice echoing in her heart. (Rossini)

21. Studer vows to kill Ramey with a sword that he gave her. (Verdi)

22. Barbieri tells Björling how her mother was burned at the stake. (Verdi)

23. Tibbett wonders whether Bori's 'infidelity' is a dream or reality. (Verdi)

24. Cretan chorus sees clear sailing for Vaness. (Mozart)

25. Baker vows that there'll be no wedding flowers. (Mozart)

ACT IV

Crostics

Operacrostic

In this puzzle, your answers to the DEFINITIONS should be entered in the spaces provided in the WORDS column, and then transferred, letter by letter, to the appropriate squares in the GRID. It is not necessary to know more than a few WORDS to begin solving. Work back and forth from the GRID to the WORDS column. A quotation will gradually begin to form in the GRID. When all the WORDS are filled in, their initial letters will spell out the author and title of the book from which the quotation is taken. Words in the GRID will often carry over from one line to the next, and the GRID is to be read horizontally, not vertically – this is not a crossword puzzle. As Wagner's Shepherd Boy says to the Pilgrims beginning their journey, 'Glück auf!'

1E	2U	3I	4M	5H		6F	7K	8S	9X	10G		11R	12Z		13A	14D	15J	16O	17b
18a	19S	20V	21Q	22W		23B	24T	25H		26L	27C	28P	29U	30B	31d	32W	33Y	34M	35G
36K		37Q	38T	39U	40I	41S	42C	43J	44J	45a	46O		47R	48Z	49P	50E	51d		52G
53A	54e	55c	56B	57U		58N	59W	60Y	61Q	62V		63e	64U	65X		66S	67X	68d	69D
70V	71Z	72T		73B	74S		75Y	76X	77Q	78I	79H	80S	81U	82R		83X	84M	85O	86L
87b	88S	89V	90T	91D	92B	93A	94T		95d	96G	97R	98I	99Z	100A	101M	102Q	103e	104b	105Z
	106X	107Y		108Z	109X		110D	111L	112T	113W	114M	115M	116C		117S	118c	119D		120T
121X	122W		123b	124G	125H	126U	127T		128Z	129C		130Z		131J	132D	133X	134G	135X	136U
137b	138A	139Q		140O	141L	142Z	143d	144M	145Q		146Z	147O	148X	149A		150D	151O	152Y	153G
154W		155W	156L		157R	158Z	159T	160a	161a		162T		163B	164W	165b	166c	167T	168Q	
169G	170Z	171B		172K	173X	174W		175R		176Q	177C	178B	179M	180R	181J		182S	183B	184Q
	185X	186U		187a	188F	189S	190M		191C	192J	193D	194U		195b	196I	197P	198H		199U
200X	201Z	202K	203E	204T	205U	206Q		207P	208T	209M	210a	211G	212C		213N	214B	215G	216M	217W
	218B	219S		220C	221R	222W	223D	224V	225J	226S	227U								

DEFINITIONS

A. Verdi protagonist who fights in Wotan's name

__ __ __ __ __ __
53 149 100 138 13 93

B. As Rodolfo puts it, 'Ma per fortuna è una _____' (3 words)

__ __ __ __ __ __ __ __ __ __ __
92 73 178 218 56 171 30 163 214 183 23

C. She 'wakes the little sleepers' (2 words)

__ __ __ __ __ __ __ __
116 42 191 129 27 177 220 212

D. Verdi's Triboulet

__ __ __ __ __ __ __ __ __
119 14 69 132 150 223 193 110 91

E. Bavarian composer of operas on Circe and Columbus

__ __ __
203 1 50

F. Texaco's roving reporter (initials)

__ __
6 188

G. He ends his opera alone at the organ

__ __ __ __ __ __ __ __ __ __
52 169 35 153 10 211 134 96 215 124

H. His 'Country Girl' awaits operatic treatment

__ __ __ __ __
79 25 198 5 125

I. How Leonora describes the wings of love (Ital.)

__ __ __ __ __
98 196 78 3 40

WORDS

J. Met baritone with movie and Hit Parade credits

<u>15</u> <u>192</u> <u>225</u> <u>131</u> <u>181</u> <u>43</u> <u>44</u>

K. Word echoed by Annina and Valzacchi

<u>36</u> <u>172</u> <u>202</u> <u>7</u>

L. Brazen-voiced baritone Titta

<u>111</u> <u>141</u> <u>26</u> <u>86</u> <u>156</u>

M. Name and title of *Aida* collaborator (2 words)

<u>114</u> <u>4</u> <u>84</u> <u>144</u> <u>216</u> <u>101</u> <u>179</u> <u>115</u> <u>34</u> <u>209</u> <u>190</u>

N. First word of Baptist's hymn, used to begin Guido's scale

<u>58</u> <u>213</u>

O. Her oxlike suitor wasn't her choice

<u>46</u> <u>85</u> <u>140</u> <u>147</u> <u>151</u> <u>16</u>

P. Disguised Windsorites in *Falstaff* Act 3

<u>49</u> <u>197</u> <u>207</u> <u>28</u>

Q. Both Rossini and Massenet wrote them

<u>145</u> <u>102</u> <u>37</u> <u>184</u> <u>61</u> <u>21</u> <u>168</u> <u>176</u> <u>206</u> <u>77</u> <u>139</u>

R. Verdi's Aquileian warrior woman

<u>11</u> <u>82</u> <u>175</u> <u>97</u> <u>221</u> <u>157</u> <u>180</u> <u>47</u>

S. Wagner's hard hats (2 words)

<u>66</u> <u>189</u> <u>88</u> <u>219</u> <u>41</u> <u>19</u>

<u>74</u> <u>182</u> <u>117</u> <u>80</u> <u>226</u> <u>8</u>

T. Heavenly Callas conductor (2 words)

<u>120</u> <u>159</u> <u>94</u> <u>167</u> <u>112</u> <u>38</u>

<u>72</u> <u>127</u> <u>208</u> <u>162</u> <u>204</u> <u>90</u> <u>24</u>

U. Driving and driven V.W. hero (3 words)

<u>64</u> <u>205</u> <u>199</u> <u>29</u> <u>126</u> <u>194</u> <u>81</u>

<u>57</u> <u>227</u> <u>186</u> <u>39</u> <u>136</u> <u>2</u>

V. Harris uncle still awaiting operatic treatment

<u>62</u> <u>70</u> <u>224</u> <u>20</u> <u>89</u>

W. Czech soprano destined for greatness (2 words)

<u>22</u> <u>113</u> <u>222</u> <u>174</u>

<u>154</u> <u>122</u> <u>217</u> <u>155</u> <u>164</u> <u>32</u> <u>59</u>

X. Operatic wife-husband team of the 1930s and 1940s (2 words)

<u>65</u> <u>135</u> <u>185</u> <u>76</u> <u>200</u> <u>106</u> <u>121</u>

<u>9</u> <u>67</u> <u>109</u> <u>83</u> <u>133</u> <u>173</u> <u>148</u>

Y. R-K hero, resists the 'Song of India'

<u>75</u> <u>33</u> <u>60</u> <u>152</u> <u>107</u>

Z. Hapless but heralded heroine in Wagner (3 words, Eng.)

<u>99</u> <u>48</u> <u>105</u> <u>158</u> <u>128</u> <u>12</u>

<u>142</u> <u>71</u> <u>201</u> <u>108</u> <u>130</u> <u>170</u> <u>146</u>

a. Put-upon but prayerful heroine in Weber

<u> </u> <u> </u> <u> </u> <u> </u> <u> </u> <u> </u>
18 160 187 210 161 45

b. Home stretch of a hectic finale

<u> </u> <u> </u> <u> </u> <u> </u> <u> </u> <u> </u> <u> </u>
195 123 17 87 165 104 137

c. Direction in which Brünnhilde speeds Sieglinde (Ger.)

<u> </u> <u> </u> <u> </u>
118 55 166

d. Met conductor Santi

<u> </u> <u> </u> <u> </u> <u> </u> <u> </u>
68 51 143 95 31

e. Virgil crowded more than four of these into less than three acts (abbrev.)

<u> </u> <u> </u> <u> </u>
103 63 54

Texaco Presents

'Texaco presents the Metropolitan Opera,' the familiar voice would intone at the start of the Saturday afternoon broadcasts that have reached opera lovers now for more than half a century. In this puzzle, with apologies to Henry and Geraldine Souvaine, to Boris Goldovsky and William Weaver, to Alberta Masiello and Mary Ellis Peltz, and all the other personalities past and present whose familiar names don't appear, I invite you to enter your answers to the DEFINITIONS in the WORDS column and then to transfer them letter by letter to the appropriate squares in the GRID, where a quotation will gradually begin to form. When the puzzle is solved, the initial letters in the WORDS column will spell out the author and title of the book from which the quotation is taken. As Leonard Warren sang on the broadcast of 3/20/43, 'Andiam. Incominciate!'

DEFINITIONS

A. Maria, shared famous intermission with Lotte Lehmann 2/2/63
110 125 31 128 60 66 12

B. Peter, Met announcer '75–
18 129 2 122 79

C. Milton, Met announcer '31–'74
42 77 6 87 55

D. Otto, helped arrange first Met broadcasts
132 44 104 8

E. Björling aria 1/11/41: 'Ah! ____, ben mio'
39 108

F. Intermission: 'Opera News ____' (3 words)
25 13 109 52 96 133 86 62

G. Corelli rafter-ringer 12/3/66 (2 words, Ital.)
4 61 112 19 106 14 92 41 23 124 68

H. Gladys, first quiz panellist 12/7/40
127 7 38 72 102 83 56 90 134

I. Most-broadcast opera for five decades
126 84 5 33

J. Lawrence, partnered H on first quiz
24 93 117 32 9 136 27

K. Met star performing locale during WWII
30 10 130

L. Francis, gave many 'Biographies in Music'
16 131 114 53 57 123 1 34

WORDS

M. Miss Upshaw, sang Susanna 1/28/95

$\overline{47}\ \overline{115}\ \overline{100}\ \overline{94}$

N. Status of Don José by end of Act 2

$\overline{101}\ \overline{17}\ \overline{118}\ \overline{58}$

O. Faust's request of Mephisto (Eng.)

$\overline{37}\ \overline{119}\ \overline{64}\ \overline{107}\ \overline{21}$

P. Pre-Met star performing locale during WWII

$\overline{76}\ \overline{20}\ \overline{50}\ \overline{135}\ \overline{85}$

Q. Most popular Texaco intermission (2 words)

$\overline{36}\ \overline{51}\ \overline{15}\ \overline{63}\ \overline{111}\ \overline{3}\ \overline{120}$

R. What questions on Q often have

$\overline{113}\ \overline{48}\ \overline{35}\ \overline{54}\ \overline{82}$

S. Sayão reached it as Manon 1/16/43 (2 words)

$\overline{89}\ \overline{43}\ \overline{95}\ \overline{28}\ \overline{74}$

T. God worshipped by Sills as Thaïs 1/28/78

$\overline{46}\ \overline{97}\ \overline{80}\ \overline{69}$

U. Cornelia _____ Skinner, quiz debut 4/19/69

$\overline{105}\ \overline{70}\ \overline{49}\ \overline{98}$

V. Kipnis reached it as Marke 2/8/41 (2 words)

$\overline{121}\ \overline{99}\ \overline{75}\ \overline{59}$

W. Mr DeLuise, broadcast debut 1/14/95

$\overline{78}\ \overline{22}\ \overline{11}$

X. Unbeatable quiz panel: ____, Mohr, Coveney

$\overline{91}\ \overline{103}\ \overline{73}\ \overline{81}\ \overline{29}\ \overline{26}$

Y. Mme Eames or Mme Calvé

$\overline{71}\ \overline{116}\ \overline{67}\ \overline{88}$

Z. '____ an earth defiled' sung by J 2/20/34

$\overline{45}\ \overline{65}\ \overline{40}$

The Tenor of His Time

Answers to the DEFINITIONS should be entered in the WORDS column and then transferred, letter by letter, to the appropriate squares in the GRID, where a quotation will gradually begin to form. Work back and forth between GRID and WORDS. When the puzzle is solved, the initial letters in the WORDS column will spell out the author and title of the book from which the quotation is taken. As Caruso once sang to Farrar, 'Vieni, vieni!'

1S	2D	3I	■	4T	5B	6Y	7G	8C	■	9Q	■	10O	11Q	12K	13U	■	14I	15K
16A	17Q	18G	19V	■	20W	21U	22Q	■	23J	24A	■	25B	26E	27V	28P	■	29L	30V
31G	■	32Y	33Z	34I	■	35O	36L	37M	38Q	39X	40Q	■	41G	42S	43Y	44J	45A	46F
47O	48Q	49B	50U	■	51G	52I	53Z	54P	■	55T	56W	■	57Q	58Z	59B	60C	61W	62I
63S	64R	■	65Z	66V	67C	■	68X	69F	70G	71H	72Z	■	73Y	74Q	■	75H	76O	77P
■	78Q	79S	80L	■	81U	82C	83X	84B	85L	■	86D	87I	■	88Q	89Z	90L	91K	92P
93A	94I	95Y	96M	97J	98V	99Y	100X	101U	102P	■	103A	104Q	105I	■	106G	107Y	108Q	109A
■	110H	111E	112Q	■	113G	114J	115T	116E	117I	■	118Q	119P	120Z	121G	122H	123K	■	124B
■	125N	126I	127Z	128Q	■	129I	130Z	131T	132L	133Q	134I	135K	136X	■	137S	138U	■	139N
140Q	141R	■	142H	143Q	144G	■	145A	146D	147M	148O	■	149D	150Q	151U	152C	■	153W	154E
■	155G	156T	157Y	■	158Q	159N	160D	161G	162K	■	163B	164O	165J	166E				

DEFINITIONS

WORDS

A. English (2 words) for C's 'La storia mia'

__ __ __ __ __ __ __
103 24 145 93 16 45 109

B. English (2 words) for C's '... è breve'

__ __ __ __ __ __ __
124 59 25 84 5 49 163

C. C sees 'una furtiva lagrima' coursing down this

__ __ __ __ __
60 82 67 8 152

D. C's fortissimo challenge in *Bohème* aria (2 words)

__ __ __ __ __
146 86 160 2 149

E. German for C's crony Scotti

__ __ __ __ __
116 154 166 26 111

F. German for what C once put in Scotti's hand on stage

__ __
69 46

G. Seven-star night for C (2 words, Fr.)

__ __ __
7 144 31

__ __ __ __ __ __ __ __ __
161 121 113 51 18 70 106 155 41

H. Did C use hip to do this from as Ramerrez?

__ __ __ __ __
122 75 110 71 142

I. December day of C's last performance (2 words)

__ __ __ __ __ __ __ __ __
14 94 134 62 52 117 105 126 87

__ __ __
3 129 34

J. C as Serse: '_____ mai fu'

<u>165</u> <u>23</u> <u>44</u> <u>114</u> <u>97</u>

K. English title for C's 1897 Giordano opera (2 words)

<u>162</u> <u>15</u> <u>135</u> <u>12</u> <u>123</u> <u>91</u>

L. C turned this in 1893

<u>132</u> <u>29</u> <u>85</u> <u>36</u> <u>90</u> <u>80</u>

M. Syllable for High B-flat in C's *Carmen* aria

<u>96</u> <u>147</u> <u>37</u>

N. Did C shoot from here as Ramerrez?

<u>125</u> <u>159</u> <u>139</u>

O. First two words of C's 1910 *Faust* quartet

<u>148</u> <u>10</u> <u>47</u> <u>35</u> <u>164</u> <u>76</u>

P. Johanna, C's first Met Aida

<u>102</u> <u>119</u> <u>54</u> <u>77</u> <u>28</u> <u>92</u>

Q. Last aria C sang in performance (4 words, Fr.)

<u>158</u> <u>11</u> <u>118</u> <u>143</u> <u>40</u> <u>108</u>

<u>38</u> <u>133</u> <u>150</u> <u>88</u> <u>78</u> <u>57</u> <u>48</u>

<u>17</u> <u>112</u> <u>9</u> <u>104</u> <u>74</u> <u>128</u> <u>140</u> <u>22</u>

R. C as Faust: 'Salut, demeure chaste _____ pure'

<u>64</u> <u>141</u>

S. Bessie, spotted C in San Francisco quake

<u>79</u> <u>63</u> <u>42</u> <u>1</u> <u>137</u>

T. December date of C's *Fanciulla* première

<u>55</u> <u>115</u> <u>131</u> <u>4</u> <u>156</u>

U. Salvatore, accompanied C on first recordings

<u>151</u> <u>21</u> <u>81</u> <u>50</u> <u>138</u> <u>101</u> <u>13</u>

V. Sembrich as Amina, to C: '_____ _____ giunge'

<u>30</u> <u>66</u> <u>98</u> <u>27</u> <u>19</u>

W. C always raised it at the Met

<u>61</u> <u>153</u> <u>56</u> <u>20</u>

X. Second word of C's first recording

<u>39</u> <u>136</u> <u>100</u> <u>68</u> <u>83</u>

Y. First word of C's first recording

<u>95</u> <u>6</u> <u>43</u> <u>99</u> <u>157</u> <u>107</u> <u>32</u> <u>73</u>

Z. C's popular 1918 recording (2 words, Eng.)

<u>89</u> <u>127</u> <u>53</u> <u>72</u>

<u>65</u> <u>33</u> <u>58</u> <u>120</u> <u>130</u>

Tenors, Baritones, and Basses

Answers to the DEFINITIONS should be entered in the WORDS column and then transferred, letter by letter, to the appropriate squares in the GRID, where a quotation will gradually begin to form. Work back and forth between GRID and WORDS. When the puzzle is solved, the initial letters in the WORDS column will spell out the author and title of the book from which the quotation is taken. As the tenor and baritone say to the bass in Così, 'Or ci divertiremo!'

1U	2D	3G	■	4I	5V	6B	■	7L	8Q	9D	10B	11U	12J	13E	14G	15S	■	16M	17V	18U	19R	20K	■
21G	22Q	23M	24U	■	25T	26I	27Q	■	28E	29L	30I	31K	32U	33T	34R	35C	36N	37E	38V	39B	■	40G	41T
■	42F	43G	44L	■	45K	46C	47J	48P	49A	■	50T	51U	52B	53V	■	54I	55K	■	56L	57M	58I	59F	60D
61J	62S	63V	64N	■	65D	66R	67E	■	68L	69T	70F	■	71R	72G	73L	74M	75B	76Q	77E	78C	79H	80F	81R
82H	■	83U	84D	85I	86E	87F	■	88B	89R	90D	■	91S	92B	93D	94K	■	95G	96B	97K	98Q	99I	100E	■
101T	102G	■	103B	104D	105U	106R	■	107S	108N	■	109E	110Q	■	111L	112U	113R	114I	■	115T	116J	117G	■	118A
119S	120I	121L	122B	123Q	124M	125P	126N	■	127M	128S	129I	130B	131U	132D	133T	134E	■	135I	136L	137B	138C	■	139N
140J	141D	■	142Q	143S	144U	145B	146I	147L	■	148D	149E	■	150R	151S	152G	153M	154K	■	155E	156T	■	157E	158U
159B	160F	161L	■	162H	163G	164U	165Q	166I	■	167V	168H	169I	170R	171T	■	172I	173M	■	174T	175U	176N	177R	■
178S	179D	180C	■	181N	182T	183F	184E	■	185J	186U	■	187G	188F	189S	190B	■	191M	192S	193V	194O	195F	196E	■
197O	198G	199T	■	200L	201V	■	202E	203I	204I	205D	206F	■	207B	208U	209D	210G	211T	212E	213V	214I	215R	216D	■

DEFINITIONS

WORDS

A. Prounoun for the subjects of this puzzle

__ __
118 49

B. *Lohengrin* line for Kollo, declaring his love (4 words)

__ __ __ __ __ __ __
137 52 39 159 10 96 103

__ __ __ __ __ __ __ __ __
92 130 6 88 190 207 75 145 122

C. Tenor classification for Araiza

__ __ __ __ __
35 138 180 46 78

D. Cilea aria for Bergonzi (4 words)

__ __ __ __ __ __ __ __ __
141 2 65 216 84 60 132 148 209

__ __ __ __ __ __
93 90 179 9 205 104

E. *Trovatore* line for Domingo, singing his farewell (5 words)

__ __ __ __ __ __ __ __ __
134 149 13 202 37 157 100 155 196

__ __ __ __ __ __ __
28 86 212 109 77 184 67

F. Donizetti tempo for Kraus

__ __ __ __ __ __ __ __ __ __
188 80 87 195 160 206 183 70 42 59

G. Gounod role for Ghiaurov

__ __ __ __ __ __ __ __
187 117 210 43 40 95 21 152

__ __ __ __ __ __
72 163 14 3 102 198

H. Dido's line for Thomas Allen's exit

__ __ __ __
168 162 79 82

I. Championship title for Pavarotti (6 words)

__ __ __ __ __ __ __ __ __
135 26 204 169 99 120 214 54 30

__ __ __ __ __ __ __ __ __
4 166 146 114 172 58 203 85 129

J. A Wotan for Wagner in the 1950s

‾‾ ‾‾ ‾‾ ‾‾ ‾‾ ‾‾
116 12 185 47 61 140

K. 'Effekt' for Bruson or Cappuccilli

‾‾ ‾‾ ‾‾ ‾‾ ‾‾ ‾‾ ‾‾
97 55 31 20 154 45 94

L. Mozart aria for Prey: 'Ein Mädchen ____

____ ,

‾‾ ‾‾ ‾‾ ‾‾
200 147 44 56

‾‾ ‾‾ ‾‾ ‾‾ ‾‾ ‾‾ ‾‾ ‾‾
111 161 29 7 121 136 73 68

M. Rossini society for Ramey

‾‾ ‾‾ ‾‾ ‾‾ ‾‾ ‾‾ ‾‾ ‾‾ ‾‾
127 16 153 191 124 173 23 74 57

N. Weber role for Weikl

‾‾ ‾‾ ‾‾ ‾‾ ‾‾ ‾‾ ‾‾
108 181 36 64 126 139 176

O. 'Auf' or 'su' for translator Porter

‾‾ ‾‾
197 194

P. Initials for Met baritone, *Faust* impresario, *Medea* composer

‾‾ ‾‾
48 125

Q. Composer of four devils for Estes, Morris, Bacquier, van Dam

‾‾ ‾‾ ‾‾ ‾‾ ‾‾ ‾‾ ‾‾ ‾‾
110 76 142 27 98 123 8 165 22

R. Gounod aria for Gedda (2 words)

‾‾ ‾‾ ‾‾ ‾‾ ‾‾
71 150 81 34 113

‾‾ ‾‾ ‾‾ ‾‾ ‾‾ ‾‾ ‾‾
177 170 215 19 89 66 106

S. Busoni role for Hampson (2 words)

‾‾ ‾‾ ‾‾ ‾‾ ‾‾ ‾‾
151 128 189 62 143 192

‾‾ ‾‾ ‾‾ ‾‾ ‾‾
178 91 119 15 107

T. *Walküre* line for Vickers, in extreme need (3 words)

‾‾ ‾‾ ‾‾ ‾‾ ‾‾ ‾‾ ‾‾ ‾‾ ‾‾ ‾‾
101 41 182 69 33 211 171 25 199 50

‾‾ ‾‾ ‾‾ ‾‾
156 133 115 174

U. *Tosca* line for Corelli, in exultation (2 words)

‾‾ ‾‾ ‾‾ ‾‾ ‾‾ ‾‾ ‾‾ ‾‾
105 32 131 11 51 144 112 1

‾‾ ‾‾ ‾‾ ‾‾ ‾‾ ‾‾ ‾‾ ‾‾
83 164 24 158 186 18 208 175

V. Rules for Jean Renoir, inspired by *Figaro* (3 words)

‾‾ ‾‾ ‾‾ ‾‾ ‾‾ ‾‾ ‾‾ ‾‾ ‾‾
193 201 63 5 53 17 213 167 38

Tutti Frutti

Answers to the DEFINITIONS should be entered in the WORDS column and then transferred, letter by letter, to the appropriate squares in the GRID, where a quotation will gradually begin to form. Work back and forth between GRID and WORDS. When the puzzle is solved, the initial letters in the WORDS column will spell out the author and title of the book from which the quotation is taken. Are you ready for *tutto*? Answer bravely, with Guglielmo, 'Tuttissimo!'

1W	2J	3C	4M	5a	6O		7U	8F	9M	10D	11X	12Z	13S	14M	15X	16E		17D	18O	19Q
	20T	21J	22R		231	24Q	25J	26Y		27U	28F	29M		30K	31S	32L	33M	34B		35J
36W		37N	38M	39S		40M	41V	42C	43G	44O	45J	46F	47Y	48M		49X	50W	51B	52I	53T
	54A	55K		56V	57F	58M	59U	60E	61J		62C	63T	64M	65X		66M	67V	68O	69Q	70Y
71H	72V		73M	74U	75D	76F		77W	78J	79A	80M		81T	82U		83M		84B	85F	86S
87G	88R	89H		90P	91K		92J	93O		94G	95M	96T	97B	98N		99R	100C		101L	102U
103S	104N	105C		106B	107W	108M		109Z	110D	111T	112U	113P	114X	115V		116Y	117M	118E		119A
120O	121X	122B	123M	124L	125a	126U	127S		128I	129M		130M	131E	132R		133T	134B		135I	136M
137Q	138G		139a	140Z	141M		142D	143N	144F		145C	146O	147M	148R	149J		150M	151J	152T	153H
154M	155K		156a	157M	158G		159F	160P		161J	162C	163B	164M	165W		166M	167L	168G	169U	170D
	171F	172T	173K	174H		175F	176E	177Y	178W		179U	180Z	181J	182M	183O	184D		185M	186A	187Y
188E	189S		190M	191D	192O	193C	194E	195W		196M	197X	198J	199F	200W		201B	202P	203M	204D
205Z	206U	207L		208Q	209I	210X	211W	212M												

DEFINITIONS

WORDS

A. G.B., the perfect Mozartite ·

79 186 119 54

B. Belmonte's beloved, Aloysia's sister

201 122 163 84 106 51 134 97 34

C. E.T.A., teller of 'Don Juan' tale

105 162 42 145 3 193 62 100

D. Mozart's fifteenth opera

17 204 142 110 191 184 75 170 10

E. Native land of 'Ochelli,' first Curzio

188 194 131 60 176 16 118

F. What Pamina will tell Sarastro (2 words, Ger.)

159 8 85

171 28 57 199 175 144 46 76

G. Hilde, an Austrian Zerlina

168 87 138 158 43 94

H. German for *tutti* or *tutte*

153 174 89 71

I. Mozart's eighth opera, _____ *Silla*

135 209 23 52 128

J. Mozart's sixteenth opera

181 2 149 161 35 25 78

61 198 92 21 45 151

K. Miss Lehmann, debuted as the Queen of
   the Night's third boy

$\overline{173}\ \overline{91}\ \overline{30}\ \overline{155}\ \overline{55}$

L. English for Da Ponte's *io voglio*

$\overline{167}\ \overline{101}\ \overline{124}\ \overline{207}\ \overline{32}$

M. Mozart's first opera (6 words, Eng.)

$\overline{164}\ \overline{38}\ \overline{108}\ \overline{196}\ \overline{9}\ \overline{182}\ \overline{80}\ \overline{123}\ \overline{4}$

$\overline{64}\ \overline{14}\ \overline{136}\ \overline{29}\ \overline{95}\ \overline{190}\ \overline{185}\ \overline{66}\ \overline{48}$

$\overline{129}\ \overline{212}\ \overline{154}\ \overline{203}\ \overline{73}\ \overline{147}\ \overline{58}\ \overline{166}\ \overline{150}$

$\overline{83}\ \overline{117}\ \overline{40}\ \overline{130}\ \overline{141}\ \overline{157}\ \overline{33}$

N. Genuine, in Salzburg

$\overline{98}\ \overline{104}\ \overline{143}\ \overline{37}$

O. Helge, a Danish Tamino

$\overline{120}\ \overline{146}\ \overline{6}\ \overline{68}\ \overline{18}\ \overline{183}\ \overline{44}\ \overline{192}\ \overline{93}$

P. Vocal range for Mozart's Apollo

$\overline{160}\ \overline{113}\ \overline{90}\ \overline{202}$

Q. Sir Donald, scholarly Mozartean

$\overline{208}\ \overline{24}\ \overline{137}\ \overline{69}\ \overline{19}$

R. What lovers do at end of Mozart's operas

$\overline{148}\ \overline{132}\ \overline{99}\ \overline{22}\ \overline{88}$

S. What lovers do to love at end of Mozart's
   operas

$\overline{189}\ \overline{39}\ \overline{86}\ \overline{31}\ \overline{103}\ \overline{13}\ \overline{127}$

T. Famous Figaro of the forties

$\overline{172}\ \overline{96}\ \overline{133}\ \overline{63}\ \overline{20}\ \overline{81}\ \overline{53}\ \overline{152}\ \overline{111}$

U. Pamina's G-minor soliloquy (3 words,
   Ger.)

$\overline{206}\ \overline{179}\ \overline{74}\ \overline{112}\ \overline{126}\ \overline{169}\ \overline{27}\ \overline{59}\ \overline{102}\ \overline{7}\ \overline{82}$

V. Roger, a French Don Giovanni

$\overline{56}\ \overline{67}\ \overline{115}\ \overline{41}\ \overline{72}$

W. Tamino's A-minor soliloquy (3 words,
   Ger.)

$\overline{195}\ \overline{165}\ \overline{1}\ \overline{50}\ \overline{178}\ \overline{36}\ \overline{200}\ \overline{77}\ \overline{107}\ \overline{211}$

X. Frank, an American Ottavio

$\overline{197}\ \overline{15}\ \overline{121}\ \overline{11}\ \overline{65}\ \overline{210}\ \overline{114}\ \overline{49}$

Y. Repeated hurrah for Almaviva's
   'generosity'

$\overline{187}\ \overline{47}\ \overline{177}\ \overline{26}\ \overline{70}\ \overline{116}$

Z. Anton, the first Idomeneo

$\overline{140}\ \overline{12}\ \overline{180}\ \overline{109}\ \overline{205}$

a. Milanov's Met Mozart role

$\overline{156}\ \overline{125}\ \overline{5}\ \overline{139}$

Napoleon Redivivus

Answers to DEFINITIONS should be entered in the WORDS column and then transferred, letter by letter, to the appropriate squares in the GRID, where a quotation will gradually begin to form. Work back and forth between GRID and WORDS. When the puzzle is solved, the initial letters in the WORDS column will spell out the author and title of the book from which the quotation is taken. As Figaro says to Rosina and her Conte, 'Presto, andiamo.'

Grid

1R	2N	3G	4Q	5I	6A	7E	8T	■	9S	10R	■	11N	12C	13G	14K	■	15B
16R	17N	■	18N	■	19U	20L	21T	■	22P	23R	24D	25G	26F	27J	28T	29U	30C
■	31N	32I	33R	■	34S	35A	36O	37B	38D	39H	40I	■	41K	42B	43S	44O	45J
■	46Q	47A	48C	49R	50N	51G	52S	■	53E	54T	■	55Q	56P	57N	■	58O	59M
60H	61G	62K	■	63M	64F	65P	■	66L	67F	68N	69H	■	70C	71S	■	72F	73P
74Q	75J	■	76K	77A	78N	79U	■	80T	81F	82M	83L	84B	■	85J	86G	■	87R
88O	89G	90D	91H	92U	■	93A	94K	95S	96J	■	97N	98G	99P	100R	101C	■	102G
103K	■	104G	105J	106A	107D	108H	109U	110I	111G	112E	113K	114Q	115N	■	116B	117J	118Q
119D	120A	121N	■	122H	123S	124E	■	125N	126T	■	127R	128Q	■	129C	130U	131N	
132E	133R	134M	■	135D	136R	137C	138N	139Q	140T	■	141B	142R	143N			

DEFINITIONS

A. Setting for R's best-known opera
93 6 106 47 120 35 77

B. Clorinda's sister (Eng.)
141 42 116 84 15 37

C. Oreste's beloved
101 30 48 137 70 129 12

D. Near victim of R's thieving magpie
90 107 24 119 17 135 38

E. First Modestina in *Il Viaggio a Reims*; adjective for B
124 7 112 53 132

F. Nino's tomb, to his ghost
64 67 26 81 72

G. First three words of *Barbiere's* last terzetto
13 98 25 89 111 51

104 102 61 3 86

H. Crucial item missing after G terzetto
108 122 91 39 69 60

I. Donizetti's adjective for R (on hearing that R wrote *Barbiere* in thirteen days)
5 32 110 40

J. Adjective for passions in *Maometto* tents
105 45 117 27 85 75 96

K. Adjective for some recent R stagings
103 94 62 14 113 41 76

L. German-Italian composer, he wrote a *Cenerentola* in 1900 (initials)
20 83 66

WORDS

M. Greek king, he made R a knight in 1843

—— —— —— ——
82 63 134 59

N. Guillaume and Hedwige, to Jemmy (3 words)

—— —— —— —— —— —— —— —— ——
121 18 131 31 57 138 2 115 11

—— —— —— —— —— ——
68 143 97 125 50 78

O. Twenty-three seats from the stage (2 words)

—— —— —— ——
36 88 58 44

P. First two words of *La Gazza Ladra*, OK?

—— —— —— —— ——
99 73 22 56 65

Q. John Wayne monicker for R's Tell

—— —— —— —— —— —— —— ——
128 46 114 4 139 74 118 55

R. Opera, to the practical R (2 words)

—— —— —— ——
10 136 23 142

—— —— —— —— —— —— —— ——
87 16 49 127 1 133 33 100

S. Nicholas, tenor friend of R

—— —— —— —— —— —— ——
9 95 34 123 43 71 52

T. Site of U.S. premieres of *Tancredi*, *Mosè*, *Italiana*, *Comte Ory* (2 words)

—— —— —— —— —— —— ——
8 126 21 140 54 28 80

U. Rosina: '____ ____ docile'

—— —— —— —— —— ——
109 29 92 79 19 130

A Dissenting View

Answers to the DEFINITIONS should be entered in the WORDS column and then transferred, letter by letter, to the appropriate squares in the GRID, where a quotation will gradually begin to form. Work back and forth from GRID to WORDS. When the puzzle is solved, the initial letters in the WORDS column will spell out the author and title of the book from which the quotation is taken. As Falstaff says to Ford, 'Passiamo insieme!'

DEFINITIONS

A. Julian wrote definitive Verdi study
146 19 83 114 44 70

B. Manrico's Act 3 cavatina (4 words)
29 126 157 2 31 98 132 227 86 147

C. Boito's best-known aria (2 words)
7 106 212 206 82 162

51 238 149 219 61

D. Siepi and Barbieri made theirs in Bing's opening *Don Carlo*
52 139 43 183 13 97

E. She names Radamès commander-in-chief
23 6 137 167

F. Otello: 'Già nella _____ _____'
30 169 214 228 89 99 130 199 36 231

G. Last two words of *Aida*, Acts 1 and 4
66 161 94 174 208 75 128

91 158 85 210

H. Renata, London mono Violetta
100 53 168 110 74 233 148

I. Along with Duncan and Fleance, mute role in *Macbeth*
235 17 125 77 189 25

J. Elvira's Act 1 aria (2 words)

 $\overline{49}$ $\overline{232}$ $\overline{140}$ $\overline{58}$ $\overline{173}$ $\overline{84}$

 $\overline{197}$ $\overline{152}$ $\overline{107}$ $\overline{202}$ $\overline{180}$ $\overline{3}$ $\overline{127}$ $\overline{241}$

K. Four of his plays made Verdi operas

 $\overline{37}$ $\overline{160}$ $\overline{143}$ $\overline{236}$ $\overline{121}$ $\overline{62}$ $\overline{108}$ $\overline{166}$

L. With M, original Shakespeare title for *Falstaff* (3 words)

 $\overline{27}$ $\overline{101}$ $\overline{194}$ $\overline{39}$ $\overline{79}$ $\overline{177}$ $\overline{215}$ $\overline{42}$

 $\overline{60}$ $\overline{226}$ $\overline{4}$ $\overline{134}$ $\overline{245}$

M. Concludes L (2 words)

 $\overline{220}$ $\overline{22}$ $\overline{109}$ $\overline{131}$ $\overline{24}$ $\overline{218}$ $\overline{111}$ $\overline{96}$ $\overline{72}$

N. Nicola, comtemporary Verdi conductor

 $\overline{129}$ $\overline{81}$ $\overline{234}$ $\overline{203}$ $\overline{14}$ $\overline{138}$ $\overline{67}$ $\overline{172}$

O. San ____, closing scene in *Don Carlo* (var.)

 $\overline{182}$ $\overline{124}$ $\overline{59}$ $\overline{141}$ $\overline{5}$

P. Original Shakespeare for Piave's 'Via, ti dico, o maledetta' (3 words)

 $\overline{32}$ $\overline{47}$ $\overline{142}$ $\overline{224}$ $\overline{15}$ $\overline{87}$ $\overline{184}$ $\overline{69}$ $\overline{192}$

 $\overline{48}$ $\overline{95}$ $\overline{229}$ $\overline{54}$

Q. Verdi's age when he began *Simon Boccanegra*

 $\overline{178}$ $\overline{35}$ $\overline{195}$ $\overline{133}$ $\overline{122}$ $\overline{155}$ $\overline{230}$ $\overline{115}$

R. Nicolai recorded *Don Carlo* with Solti and Karajan

 $\overline{68}$ $\overline{28}$ $\overline{170}$ $\overline{46}$ $\overline{112}$ $\overline{16}$ $\overline{150}$ $\overline{175}$

S. English for Verdi's 'lo giuro' (3 words)

 $\overline{50}$ $\overline{80}$ $\overline{190}$ $\overline{239}$ $\overline{38}$ $\overline{163}$

T. Joseph designed Met *Traviata, Don Carlo, Falstaff* for Gatti

 $\overline{209}$ $\overline{10}$ $\overline{117}$ $\overline{55}$ $\overline{113}$

U. Joan, London stereo Violetta

 $\overline{65}$ $\overline{116}$ $\overline{164}$ $\overline{21}$ $\overline{222}$ $\overline{154}$ $\overline{57}$ $\overline{244}$ $\overline{223}$ $\overline{200}$

V. Otello's shout after the storm

 $\overline{11}$ $\overline{88}$ $\overline{179}$ $\overline{135}$ $\overline{171}$ $\overline{153}$ $\overline{34}$ $\overline{119}$

W. Adjective for tenor Domingo and his *Luisa Miller* aria

 $\overline{40}$ $\overline{136}$ $\overline{64}$ $\overline{45}$ $\overline{105}$ $\overline{185}$

X. Role for *premier basse* in *Don Carlos*

 $\overline{78}$ $\overline{225}$ $\overline{56}$ $\overline{181}$ $\overline{159}$ $\overline{1}$ $\overline{104}$ $\overline{71}$

Y. Her Aida opened Met's Gatti era (2 words)

 $\overline{102}$ $\overline{123}$ $\overline{18}$ $\overline{213}$

 $\overline{120}$ $\overline{243}$ $\overline{188}$ $\overline{12}$ $\overline{216}$ $\overline{145}$ $\overline{205}$

Z. Falstaff: 'Va, ____ John'

 $\overline{193}$ $\overline{217}$ $\overline{92}$ $\overline{20}$ $\overline{76}$ $\overline{156}$ $\overline{191}$

a. Desdemona's hand knew no trace 'del duolo e dell' ____'

 $\overline{176}$ $\overline{118}$ $\overline{144}$

b. Nicola recorded *Don Carlo* with Previtali

<u> </u> <u> </u> <u> </u> <u> </u> <u> </u>
26 93 237 201 8

<u> </u> <u> </u> <u> </u> <u> </u> <u> </u> <u> </u>
90 186 103 165 240 207

c. First two words of Fenton's aria

<u> </u> <u> </u> <u> </u> <u> </u> <u> </u> <u> </u> <u> </u> <u> </u> <u> </u>
242 198 41 211 73 221 9 187 204

d. Monks' chorus in *Don Carlo*: '____ ____ spuntò'

<u> </u> <u> </u> <u> </u> <u> </u>
151 63 196 33

Verdi on Wagner

Answers to the DEFINITIONS should be entered in the WORDS column and then transferred, letter by letter, to the appropriate squares in the GRID, where a quotation will gradually begin to form. Work back and forth between GRID and WORDS. When the puzzle is solved, the initial letters in the WORDS column will spell out the author and title of the book from which the quotation is taken. As Sam says to Tom, 'Andiam!'

1M	2J	3D	4B	■	5E	■	6A	7C	8Q	9Y	10J	■	11U	12S	13B	■	14Z	15R	16I	17S	18Q	■	19B
20H	■	21I	22C	23F	24K	25Y	26L	27E	■	28S	29B	30N	31T	32G	■	33E	34V	35B	36M	37Y	■	38J	39W
40I	41K	42F	43L	44P	■	45I	46O	■	47R	48Y	49N	■	50T	51A	52Q	53Y	54W	■	55C	56Y	57O	58K	59P
■	60X	61H	62U	63G	64V	65Y	66B	■	67O	68W	69Z	■	70S	71K	72U	73M	■	74R	75S	76O	77T	78U	■
79N	80C	81Z	82S	83B	84T	■	85K	86Z	87S	88C	89Y	90Q	91B	■	92B	93M	■	94I	95B	96F	97X	98U	99C
100D	101I	■	102R	103W	104I	105J	106K	107Z	108F	109U	110H	111B	■	112U	113Y	■	114F	115Y	116B	117E	118N	119J	120I
■	121B	122Z	123T	124N	■	125D	126X	127U	128E	129Y	130P	131F	132B	■	133Q	134Y	135N	136L	137T	138J	139Q	140M	141K
■	142B	143Z	144A	145H	146E	■	147K	148D	■	149D	150V	151Q	152T	■	153K	154Q	155A	■	156X	157E	158V	159Z	■
160R	161Y	162C	163W	164M	■	165R	166J	167K	168T	■	169E	170Z	171N	172C	173I	174B	175W	176I	177A	178X	179B	180T	■
181A	182N	183X	■	184K	185F	186B	■	187N	188Q	189K	■	190Q	■	191U	192N	193Y	194J	195L	■	196J	197A	198N	199F
200G	201T	■	202C	203B	204N	205B	206K	■	207I	208J	209Y	210K	211P	212V	213F	214U	215A	216G	■	217K	218Q	219T	220O
■	221N	222V	■	223D	224K	225X	■	226B	227C	228R	229Q	230G	231G	232V	233J	234A	■	235B	236R	237D	■	238H	239S
240Y	241N	242F	243O	244Q	■	245H	246F	■	247D	■	248I	249L	250B	251I	252D	■	253H	254M	255B	256F	257J	■	■

DEFINITIONS

A. Sparafucile's sister

B. Wagner treatise: A ____ ____ ____ ____ (Eng.)

C. Verdi duet: '____ ____ ____ brivido'

D. *Neu inszeniert* (2 words, Eng.)

E. Renato and Sparafucile (Ital.)

F. Age of both Verdi and Wagner by end of October 1841

G. Morold's betrothed

H. Two verbs for *Tristan*'s orchestral sea

I. Comprimario role in Y (2 words, Eng.)

WORDS

— — — — — — — — —
177 6 234 155 181 144 51 215 197

— — — — — — — — —
226 19 250 92 203 4 116 132 235

— — — — — — — —
121 255 29 179 205 35 13 83

— — — — — — —
142 95 174 186 111 66 91

— — — — — — — — — —
227 202 88 22 80 7 172 162 55 99

— — — — — — — — —
252 3 223 100 149 247 125 148 237

— — — — — — — — —
169 146 33 128 27 117 5 199 157

— — — — — —
242 185 42 256 114 246

— — — — —
96 131 23 213 108

— — — — — —
231 32 200 63 216 230

— — — — — — —
61 253 245 20 145 110 238

— — — — —
120 16 94 248 101

— — — — — — — —
21 251 45 207 176 104 40 173

J. Verdi's 'Anvil Chorus' (3 words, Ital.)

<u>196</u> <u>2</u> <u>105</u> <u>10</u> <u>233</u> <u>194</u>

<u>257</u> <u>166</u> <u>138</u> <u>119</u> <u>38</u> <u>208</u>

K. How Offenbach might have titled Wagner's best-known treatise (3 words, Eng.)

<u>71</u> <u>210</u> <u>141</u> <u>106</u> <u>206</u> <u>167</u> <u>217</u> <u>85</u>

<u>224</u> <u>24</u> <u>189</u> <u>58</u> <u>41</u> <u>184</u> <u>147</u> <u>153</u>

L. Jacques, a stentorian Tristan

<u>249</u> <u>26</u> <u>195</u> <u>136</u> <u>43</u>

M. It first saw *Tristan*, with Niemann and Lehmann, in 1886

<u>164</u> <u>254</u> <u>1</u> <u>93</u> <u>36</u> <u>140</u> <u>73</u>

N. Wagner hero's name and pseudonym (2 words)

<u>118</u> <u>30</u> <u>221</u> <u>49</u> <u>241</u> <u>187</u> <u>182</u>

<u>171</u> <u>79</u> <u>198</u> <u>192</u> <u>135</u> <u>204</u> <u>124</u>

O. Verdians Bastianini and Panizza

<u>243</u> <u>67</u> <u>220</u> <u>46</u> <u>57</u> <u>76</u>

P. Wagner ride: 'Walküren____'

<u>211</u> <u>59</u> <u>130</u> <u>44</u>

Q. Ernestine, a monumental Brangäne

<u>133</u> <u>229</u> <u>18</u> <u>139</u> <u>151</u> <u>52</u> <u>154</u> <u>244</u>

<u>218</u> <u>90</u> <u>190</u> <u>188</u> <u>8</u>

R. Meditative baritone solo from Y (2 words, Ger.)

<u>74</u> <u>160</u> <u>47</u> <u>236</u> <u>165</u> <u>102</u> <u>15</u> <u>228</u>

S. Tristan: '____ ____ ____ ich von je gewesen'

<u>12</u> <u>17</u> <u>75</u> <u>70</u> <u>82</u> <u>239</u> <u>28</u> <u>87</u>

T. Joseph, first Rienzi and Tannhäuser

<u>180</u> <u>123</u> <u>137</u> <u>50</u> <u>219</u> <u>201</u> <u>84</u> <u>77</u> <u>168</u>

<u>152</u> <u>31</u>

U. Bass role in *Nabucco* or *Aida* (2 words)

<u>11</u> <u>109</u> <u>127</u> <u>78</u> <u>62</u> <u>72</u> <u>112</u> <u>214</u> <u>191</u> <u>98</u>

V. Riccardo and Gilda, encountering E (Ital.)

<u>232</u> <u>150</u> <u>34</u> <u>222</u> <u>64</u> <u>158</u> <u>212</u>

W. Verdian Miss Mason and Wagnerian Miss Coates

<u>39</u> <u>103</u> <u>163</u> <u>54</u> <u>68</u> <u>175</u>

X. Act 1 *Traviata* chorus: 'Si ____'

<u>60</u> <u>126</u> <u>183</u> <u>178</u> <u>225</u> <u>156</u> <u>97</u>

Y. Wagner opera Verdi thought 'fine in a German environment. Here in Italy, no.'

<u>37</u> <u>193</u> <u>9</u> <u>209</u> <u>56</u> <u>240</u> <u>113</u> <u>134</u> <u>25</u> <u>115</u>

<u>89</u> <u>48</u> <u>129</u> <u>161</u> <u>65</u> <u>53</u>

Z. English for S (3 words)

<u>143</u> <u>81</u> <u>107</u> <u>170</u> <u>14</u> <u>122</u> <u>159</u> <u>86</u> <u>69</u>

His Master's Voice

Answers to the DEFINITIONS should be entered in the WORDS column, and then transferred, letter by letter, to the appropriate squares in the GRID, where a quotation will gradually begin to form. Work back and forth from GRID to WORDS. When the puzzle is solved, the initial letters in the WORDS column will spell out the author and title of the book from which the quotation is taken. As the pageboys sing to Wolfram, 'Beginne.'

1M	2D	3U	4R	5Q	6e	7X	■	8P	9K	10N	■	11O	12S	13J	14X	15H	16U	17L	18V	19W
20Z	21T	22Y	23d	■	24G	25E	26A	27C	■	28I	29B	30I	31F	32a	·	33S	34b	35L	36P	37N
38e	■	39c	40O	41d	42E	43C	■	44a	45b	46K	47B	48M	49X	■	50G	51c	52P	53F	54b	55M
■	56e	57J	58A	■	59T	60O	61V	62D	63R	64d	65H	66L	■	67L	68b	■	69d	70A	71E	72K
73c	74W	75B	76d	77Z	78R	79T	■	80C	81D	82X	83O	■	84e	85P	86d	■	87I	88P	89a	90R
91U	92b	93N	94B	95X	96b	■	97X	98F	99b	100D	101H	■	102T	103X	104L	105A	■	106P	■	107Z
108d	109E	110a	111F	112L	113W	■	114R	115X	116a	117L	118B	119Z	120C	121a	122P	123J	■	124I	125a	■
126A	127Z	128C	129J	130S	131T	132G	133C	■	134U	135d	■	136X	■	137J	138I	139T	140F	141Y	■	142P
143Y	144V	145O	146e	■	147E	148a	■	149R	150b	151Y	152I	■	153Z	154J	155E	156L	■	157b	158V	159K
■	160Q	161O	162B	163c	164H	165d	■	166P	167K	168U	169P	170L	■	171V	172d	173E	■	174W	175U	176Z
177c	178B	■	179T	180J	181b	182D	183X	■	184G	185N	186K	■	187X	188J	189e	190A	■	191D	192I	■
193P	194a	195J	196Y	■	197a	198U	■	199b	200G	201M	■	202G	203b	204I	205U	206c	■	207D	208I	209c
210R	211E	212J	■	213W	214F	■	215S	216R	217e	218L	■	219M	220a	221b	222A	223M	224K	225G	226Y	
227O	228C	■	229F	230I	231M	232O	■	233a	234O	235C	■	236b	237H	238b	■					

DEFINITIONS

A. Zerlina puts his hand on her heart

105 222 58 190 26 126 70

B. Elektra escorts him to his death

94 29 178 75 118 162 47

C. Ship from which Billy was painlessly impressed: *The* ____ ____ *Man*

43 128 133 27 80 235 120 228

D. Günther, a Siegmund of the 1950s

191 62 2 100 132 81 207

E. Broadway Kate's misandristic aria (3 words)

25 147 155 173 211 71 42 109

F. Mozart introduces him with three trombones

53 214 229 31 111 140 98

G. Met Miss Jones

202 24 184 132 225 50 200

H. Beethoven's jailer of Seville

164 237 15 65 101

I. Dutch conductor in Bayreuth and San Francisco

204 28 192 87 230 152 30 208 138 124

J. The seven-year-old Donati

137 154 13 212 188 195 123 57 129 180

K. The slayer of Laius

167 159 224 9 72 186 46

WORDS

L. Brünnhilde's three words at depth of Immolation Scene (Ger.)

<u> </u> <u> </u> <u> </u> <u> </u> <u> </u> <u> </u> <u> </u> <u> </u> <u> </u> <u> </u>
112 117 66 218 170 17 35 104 156 67

M. How Ottavio's peace relates to Anna's

<u> </u> <u> </u> <u> </u> <u> </u> <u> </u> <u> </u> <u> </u>
1 201 231 48 223 219 55

N. Original Greek name for Gluck's Amor

<u> </u> <u> </u> <u> </u> <u> </u>
37 93 185 10

O. He's slain with an arrow by Strauss's Apollo

<u> </u> <u> </u> <u> </u> <u> </u> <u> </u> <u> </u> <u> </u> <u> </u> <u> </u>
145 40 161 83 234 60 11 227 232

P. Central section of *Tristan's* Act 2 (Ger.)

<u> </u> <u> </u> <u> </u> <u> </u> <u> </u> <u> </u>
169 52 122 193 88 142

<u> </u> <u> </u> <u> </u> <u> </u> <u> </u>
36 106 166 8 85

Q. First word of *The Mikado*

<u> </u> <u> </u>
5 160

R. First soloist in *The Mikado*

<u> </u> <u> </u> <u> </u> <u> </u> <u> </u> <u> </u> <u> </u> <u> </u>
210 114 216 149 90 4 78 63

S. Eleven seats from the stage (2 words)

<u> </u> <u> </u> <u> </u> <u> </u>
12 215 33 130

T. First word of Iago's *brindisi* (Ital.)

<u> </u> <u> </u> <u> </u> <u> </u> <u> </u> <u> </u> <u> </u>
131 79 139 179 102 21 59

U. Ileana from Romania

<u> </u> <u> </u> <u> </u> <u> </u> <u> </u> <u> </u> <u> </u> <u> </u>
16 134 198 175 168 91 205 3

V. Melancholy miner at The Polka

<u> </u> <u> </u> <u> </u> <u> </u> <u> </u>
158 144 18 61 171

W. Wells Fargo agent at The Polka

<u> </u> <u> </u> <u> </u> <u> </u> <u> </u>
19 74 213 174 113

X. Isolde's three words at height of vengeance aria (Ger.)

<u> </u> <u> </u> <u> </u> <u> </u> <u> </u> <u> </u> <u> </u>
103 136 115 183 7 95 82 49

<u> </u> <u> </u> <u> </u>
97 14 187

Y. Position of Hylas's ship in *Les Troyens*

<u> </u> <u> </u> <u> </u> <u> </u> <u> </u> <u> </u>
141 22 143 196 151 226

Z. Strauss said of her Salome: 'We succeeded in spite of Auntie ____.'

<u> </u> <u> </u> <u> </u> <u> </u> <u> </u> <u> </u> <u> </u>
153 176 119 20 77 107 127

a. Manrico's song from the tower (4 words, Ital.)

<u> </u> <u> </u> <u> </u> <u> </u> <u> </u> <u> </u> <u> </u>
194 233 116 32 148 89 197

<u> </u> <u> </u> <u> </u> <u> </u> <u> </u>
121 125 44 110 220

b. Only Wagner opera with a prologue

<u> </u> <u> </u> <u> </u> <u> </u> <u> </u> <u> </u>
54 68 157 199 92 181

<u> </u> <u> </u> <u> </u> <u> </u> <u> </u> <u> </u> <u> </u> <u> </u>
236 34 99 221 96 203 45 150 238

c. Sword left for one in need

<u> </u> <u> </u> <u> </u> <u> </u> <u> </u> <u> </u> <u> </u>
39 73 206 51 163 177 209

d. Adjective for Sir Geraint's 'Il Sogno'

<u> </u> <u> </u> <u> </u> <u> </u> <u> </u> <u> </u> <u> </u> <u> </u> <u> </u>
165 41 64 23 172 86 69 108 135 76

e. Hans, a seismic Wagner conductor

<u> </u> <u> </u> <u> </u> <u> </u> <u> </u> <u> </u>
38 84 217 56 6 146 189

It's in the Cards

Answers to the DEFINITIONS should be entered in the WORDS column, and then transferred, letter by letter, to the appropriate squares in the GRID, where a quotation will gradually begin to form. Work back and forth between GRID and WORDS. When the puzzle is solved, the initial letters in the WORDS column will spell out the author and title of the book from which the quotation is taken. As the smugglers in *Carmen* sing confidently, 'Marchons!'

1Q	2D		3L	4H		5C	6B	7J	8S		9N	10L	11P	12D	13O	14X	15B		16G	17W	18N	19E	
20F	21K	22I	23Q	24A		25P	26O	27W	28P	29I		30A	31Y	32S	33W	34C		35A	36N	37J	38M	39P	
40Y	41I		42N	43T	44Q	45G		46T		47A	48S	49X	50K	51C		52T	53E		54F	55M	56T	57N	58K
59R		60J	61O	62C		63S	64P		65R	66L		67X	68Q	69I		70C	71X		72D	73S	74E		75S
76H	77P	78M		79U	80Q	81I	82R	83T	84U	85P	86Y	87X	88J		89E	90X	91R	92O	93D		94E	95A	96J
97W		98O	99B	100T	101W	102Y	103O	104B		105G	106I		107V	108S	109P		110H	111Q		112V	113A	114W	115D
	116I	117R	118Q	119N	120L		121O	122X	123J		124B	125Z	126L		127T	128X	129B	130J	131Q	132V	133P		134A
135S		136I	137Z	138P		139E	140D	141J	142K	143C	144Z		145B	146X	147A		148L	149Z		150B	151N	152X	153C
154R	155E		156L	157J	158S		159K	160M	161T	162D		163A		164M	165L	166H	167F		168F	169X		170G	171O
172I		173K	174T	175Z	176A		177P		178S	179Q	180R	181H		182C	183X	184U		185O	186I	187Q		188K	189A
190P	191L	192X	193I	194T	195S	196O		197L	198E	199O		200R	201P	202C	203A	204Y	205M	206R	207Q		208A	209B	
210J	211O	212D	213K	214J	215N		216I	217W	218I	219Z	220N	221B	222J	223I		224Y	225G	226P		227H	228V	229Y	
230I	231J	232Q	233R	234K		235D	236T	237O	238E	239V		240T	241X	242J	243P	244S	245U	246F	247G	248L	249B		

DEFINITIONS

A. Henri Meilhac's collaborator

‾35‾ ‾189‾ ‾30‾ ‾134‾ ‾113‾ ‾208‾ ‾47‾

‾176‾ ‾163‾ ‾203‾ ‾147‾ ‾95‾ ‾24‾

B. Met Carmen of the 1950s

‾99‾ ‾129‾ ‾145‾ ‾15‾

‾249‾ ‾124‾ ‾150‾ ‾221‾ ‾6‾ ‾104‾ ‾209‾

C. Irina, Bolshoi Carmen of the 1950s

‾34‾ ‾62‾ ‾51‾ ‾153‾ ‾143‾ ‾202‾ ‾70‾ ‾5‾ ‾182‾

D. Gladys, Met Carmen of the 1940s

‾93‾ ‾212‾ ‾12‾ ‾115‾ ‾2‾ ‾162‾ ‾235‾ ‾140‾ ‾72‾

E. Miss Alarie, Montreal Micaëla

‾139‾ ‾198‾ ‾74‾ ‾155‾ ‾89‾ ‾238‾ ‾53‾ ‾19‾ ‾94‾

F. Vocal ensemble for *Carmen* Act 3 finale

‾168‾ ‾54‾ ‾246‾ ‾20‾ ‾167‾

G. Caruso as José sang '____ ____ di nel carcero oscuro'

‾105‾ ‾225‾ ‾16‾ ‾170‾ ‾45‾ ‾247‾

H. Carmen's first words to José in Act 4 (Eng., 2 words)

‾110‾ ‾227‾ ‾4‾ ‾181‾ ‾76‾ ‾166‾

I. 'Votre toast' (Eng., 3 words)

‾136‾ ‾186‾ ‾22‾ ‾230‾ ‾172‾ ‾216‾ ‾69‾ ‾29‾

‾223‾ ‾106‾ ‾116‾ ‾218‾ ‾41‾ ‾193‾ ‾81‾

J. Carmen Jones's movie Joe

‾‾ ‾‾ ‾‾ ‾‾ ‾‾
231 242 123 7 214

‾‾ ‾‾ ‾‾ ‾‾ ‾‾ ‾‾ ‾‾ ‾‾ ‾‾
141 222 88 210 60 157 37 130 96

K. All-time greatest Carmen?

‾‾ ‾‾ ‾‾ ‾‾ ‾‾ ‾‾ ‾‾ ‾‾ ‾‾
58 173 159 188 50 213 142 21 234

L. Bizet's collaborators, Italian style

‾‾ ‾‾ ‾‾ ‾‾ ‾‾ ‾‾ ‾‾ ‾‾
165 191 197 248 126 10 120 148

‾‾ ‾‾ ‾‾
66 156 3

M. First month in Phillips's *The Carmen Chronicle*

‾‾ ‾‾ ‾‾ ‾‾ ‾‾ ‾‾
55 160 38 205 164 78

N. Beecham, Los Angeles *Carmen* conductor (2 words)

‾‾ ‾‾ ‾‾ ‾‾ ‾‾ ‾‾ ‾‾ ‾‾ ‾‾
9 151 220 42 119 36 57 18 215

O. 'La fleur que tu m'avais jetée' (Eng., 3 words)

‾‾ ‾‾ ‾‾ ‾‾ ‾‾ ‾‾ ‾‾ ‾‾ ‾‾
185 237 92 121 211 171 98 103 26

‾‾ ‾‾ ‾‾ ‾‾
196 61 13 199

P. The 'Seguidilla' (Fr., 3 words)

‾‾ ‾‾ ‾‾ ‾‾ ‾‾ ‾‾ ‾‾
25 243 109 39 190 138 77

‾‾ ‾‾ ‾‾ ‾‾ ‾‾ ‾‾ ‾‾ ‾‾
226 85 28 201 177 11 64 133

Q. Met Carmen of the 1960s

‾‾ ‾‾ ‾‾ ‾‾ ‾‾ ‾‾
232 187 118 1 80 179

‾‾ ‾‾ ‾‾ ‾‾ ‾‾ ‾‾
23 207 111 68 131 44

R. U.S. mezzo, sang soprano in the 1960s (2 words)

‾‾ ‾‾ ‾‾ ‾‾ ‾‾ ‾‾ ‾‾ ‾‾ ‾‾ ‾‾
65 82 233 59 154 180 200 91 117 206

S. Met Carmen of the 1970s

‾‾ ‾‾ ‾‾ ‾‾ ‾‾ ‾‾ ‾‾
75 244 48 63 178 8 108

‾‾ ‾‾ ‾‾ ‾‾ ‾‾
73 158 135 32 195

T. 'Crushed-in' effect at the beginning of the 'Chanson bohème'

‾‾ ‾‾ ‾‾ ‾‾ ‾‾ ‾‾ ‾‾ ‾‾
46 127 161 100 52 240 194 43

‾‾ ‾‾ ‾‾ ‾‾
236 174 56 83

U. It draws a tear at the end of *Carmen*?

‾‾ ‾‾ ‾‾ ‾‾
184 79 245 84

V. Dominant colour in *Carmen* sets?

‾‾ ‾‾ ‾‾ ‾‾ ‾‾
107 132 228 239 112

W. Which of prima donnas R or Z sang Carmen at the Met?

‾‾ ‾‾ ‾‾ ‾‾ ‾‾ ‾‾ ‾‾
33 217 27 101 17 114 97

X. 'Huit clos,' unwelcome sign for smugglers (2 words)

‾‾ ‾‾ ‾‾ ‾‾ ‾‾ ‾‾ ‾‾ ‾‾ ‾‾ ‾‾
183 67 152 241 90 169 122 87 14 146

‾‾ ‾‾ ‾‾ ‾‾
71 49 128 192

Y. Appropriate marking for José/Micaëla duet:
con _____

<u> </u> <u> </u> <u> </u> <u> </u> <u> </u> <u> </u> <u> </u>
204 86 224 229 102 40 31

Z. Marianne, German soprano, sang mezzo in
the 1960s

<u> </u> <u> </u> <u> </u> <u> </u> <u> </u> <u> </u>
149 144 137 219 175 125

Depravity

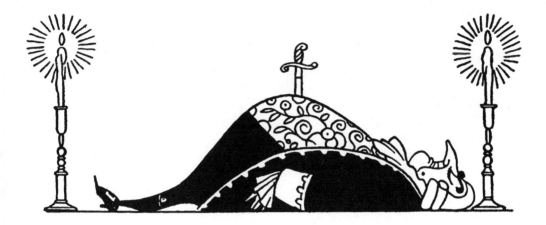

Answers to the DEFINITIONS should be entered in the WORDS column and then transferred, letter by letter, to the appropriate square in the GRID, where a quotation will gradually begin to form. Work back and forth between GRID and WORDS. When the puzzle is solved, the initial letters in the WORDS column will spell out the author and title of the book from which the quotation is taken. As Tosca says (too late!) to her Mario, 'Presto, andiam!'

1A	2J	3P	4K	5O		6N	7I	8R	9C		10W	11S	12N	13P	14T	15E		16O	17P	18J
19M	20O	21W		22T	23K	24R	25P	26G	27O	28E		29W	30R		31C	32U		33R	34X	35A
36S	37L		38N	39D	40I	41X	42C	43O	44H		45F	46B	47E	48W	49R	50K	51C	52T		53J
54M	55S	56R	57E	58F		59D	60V		61L	62P	63H		64S	65W	66O	67R	68M	69U	70T	
71L	72J		73H	74M	75P		76R	77C	78S	79L	80O	81N	82V	83B		84J	85I		86H	87C
	88X	89Q	90P	91O	92S	93G		94W	95I	96R	97K		98E	99T	100P	101F	102G	103H	104S	105P
	106L	107R		108E	109O	110N	111D	112C	113L	114K	115A		116B	117E	118X	119I	120O	121N		122U
123W	124D	125C		126P	127J		128R	129C		130Q		131E	132M	133R	134I		135F	136O	137K	138M
	139W	140B	141P	142L		143T	144H	145N	146I	147V	148O	149R	150V		151E	152S	153X		154W	155E
156D		157N	158R	159A	160J	161P	162O	163D	164C	165D		166G	167W		168O	169R	170B	171T	172U	173D
174M	175O	176I		177S	178F	179P	180X	181V	182O											

DEFINITIONS

WORDS

A. Trulove in Bedlam: 'God is merciful and
_____'

— — — —
159 35 115 1

B. Gluck hero

— — — — —
46 170 116 83 140

C. Author puts him in 'the significant operatic
canon'

— — — — — — — — — —
87 9 42 77 164 112 31 129 125 51

D. Gluck heroine

— — — — — — — —
165 173 124 59 39 163 111 156

E. Author quotes from Bentley's *The* _____ *as
Thinker*

— — — — — — — — — —
108 57 151 15 47 28 117 131 155 98

F. This Joseph wrote an opera on B and D

— — — — —
178 101 58 135 45

G. Kundry: 'Ich sah das _____'

— — — —
26 166 102 93

H. What author did for *19th Century Music*

— — — — — —
63 103 86 73 144 44

I. Petruchio: 'Were thine the _____ grace'

— — — — — — — —
146 7 176 85 95 40 119 134

J. Author calls him 'a sensationalist in the old
style'

— — — — — — —
53 160 72 2 127 18 84

K. Author says it may be 'the most beautiful
number ... in the whole of opera' (2 words,
Ital.)

— — — — — —
137 23 97 50 4 114

L. Author credits this as source for *Aida*

—— —— —— —— —— —— ——
113 71 37 79 142 61 106

M. Author details Verdi's 'unique transformation' of this source

—— —— —— —— —— —— ——
54 19 74 68 138 174 132

N. Last word of *Falstaff* Act 2

—— —— —— —— —— —— —— ——
145 12 121 38 6 81 157 110

O. Author: 'The orchestra screams the first thing that comes into its head, ____' (4 words, Ital.)

—— —— —— —— —— —— —— ——
27 16 109 168 91 148 5 182

—— —— —— —— —— —— —— ——
175 80 120 162 43 66 20 136

P. Composers, contemporaries of Verdi (2 words, Eng.)

—— —— —— —— ——
141 17 161 25 126

—— —— —— —— —— —— —— ——
13 100 179 105 62 75 90 3

Q. Initials for Violetta's lover or for a famous Violetta

—— ——
130 89

R. Violetta's last-act aria (3 words, Ital.)

—— —— —— —— —— —— —— ——
169 49 158 128 24 33 149 67

—— —— —— —— —— —— ——
76 8 30 107 96 56 133

S. Critic Harold C.

—— —— —— —— —— —— —— —— ——
55 177 11 104 152 36 92 78 64

T. Author puts him in 'the significant operatic canon'

—— —— —— —— —— —— ——
143 171 14 99 22 52 70

U. Six seats from the stage (2 words)

—— —— —— ——
69 32 122 172

V. Campra or Cluytens

—— —— —— —— ——
147 60 150 82 181

W. Librettist of L

—— —— —— —— —— —— —— —— —— ——
139 21 154 65 10 94 48 167 29 123

X. Tom in Bedlam: 'Forgive ____ and he shall faithful prove'

—— —— —— —— —— ——
88 153 34 118 41 180

Facing the Enigmas

Answers to the DEFINITIONS should be entered in the WORDS column, and then transferred, letter by letter, to the appropriate squares in the GRID, where a quotation will gradually begin to form. Work back and forth from GRID to WORDS. When the puzzle is solved, the initial letters in the WORDS column will spell out the author and title of the book from which the quotation is taken. As the people of Peking say to Prince Calaf when he faces the enigmas, 'Coraggio!'

1L	2c	3A	4H	5M		6Q	7N	8V	9I	10T	11J	12R	13W	14D		15C	16b	17J	18K
	19I	20P	21R	22W		23C	24J	25U		26F	27d	28A	29L	30g		31U	32R	33c	34S
35Q	36L		37W	38Y	39M		40L	41B	42H	43Y	44a	45f		46S	47L	48Z		49g	50M
51f	52N	53Z	54b		55J	56f	57F	58Z		59G	60g	61Y	62Z	63H		64Y	65C	66O	
67F	68f	69T	70e		71P	72E	73d	74L	75Q	76g	77L		78X	79g		80b	81R	82N	
83I	84b	85P	86K		87S	88g	89D	90V	91J		92L	93L	94P	95R	96J	97Z		98I	99Z
100J		101K	102L	103W	104b	105B	106e	107U		108b	109I	110T		111E	112a	113d		114g	115G
116J	117d		118I	119f	120W	121D	122O	123X	124U		125g	126U	127W	128b	129T		130D	131d	
132P	133c	134Q	135R	136f	137Y	138T		139Z	140N	141Y		142e	143F	144V	145F		146C	147L	148D
149H	150b		151A	152R		153g	154P	155L		156W	157K	158b		159c	160b		161X	162N	163S
	164G	165L	166Q	167J	168W		169H	170c	171c		172Y	173C	174d	175K	176F	177H		178I	179d
180R	181T	182V	183W	184Z		185I	186a	187S	188J	189O	190Z	191T		192J	193R	194H	195c		196Y
197J	198d	199R	200P		201X	202U		203F	204S	205J		206M	207I	208P	209I		210J	211D	212d
213H	214I	215R	216E		217M	218Z	219I	220D	221J	222I	223G	224R							

DEFINITIONS

WORDS

A. First word of Renato's aria

___ ___ ___
3   28 151

B. Second word of Renato's aria

___ ___
105 41

C. Lily Pons kept Met in suspense awaiting it
(2 words)

___ ___ ___ ___ ___
15 173 146 65 23

D. It allots $40 million annually to its national opera

___ ___ ___ ___ ___ ___ ___
220 211 14 130 89 148 121

E. Prop for *Peter Grimes* or *Pearl Fishers*

___ ___ ___
111 216 72

F. *Née* Kunc, she had 'one of the most beautiful
voices of the century'

___ ___ ___ ___ ___ ___ ___
26 176 145 203 57 67 143

G. His favourite song was 'Ohne mich'

___ ___ ___ ___
223 59 115 164

H. Favourite song for Marie or Preziosilla

___ ___ ___ ___ ___ ___ ___ ___
213 169 177 4 42 194 63 149

I. Moore had him beat the devil (2 words)

___ ___ ___ ___ ___ ___
222 9 178 207 209 83

___ ___ ___ ___ ___ ___ ___
98 214 19 118 185 109 219

J. 1890 Met subscribers petitioned against its repetition (3 words)

$\overline{11}\ \overline{197}\ \overline{116}\ \overline{221}\ \overline{96}\ \overline{17}\ \overline{192}\ \overline{188}$

$\overline{210}\ \overline{100}\ \overline{205}\ \overline{91}\ \overline{167}\ \overline{55}\ \overline{24}$

K. Setting for an opera each by Mozart, Rossini, Verdi, Strauss

$\overline{18}\ \overline{175}\ \overline{157}\ \overline{101}\ \overline{86}$

L. Mastersinger who sends regrets via apprentice (2 words, Eng.)

$\overline{77}\ \overline{29}\ \overline{92}\ \overline{36}\ \overline{165}\ \overline{74}\ \overline{93}\ \overline{40}$

$\overline{47}\ \overline{102}\ \overline{1}\ \overline{155}\ \overline{147}$

M. They behave like Fiordiligi and Dorabella (Ital.)

$\overline{206}\ \overline{50}\ \overline{5}\ \overline{217}\ \overline{39}$

N. Julius often responded to Melchior's 'Alte Weise'

$\overline{162}\ \overline{7}\ \overline{82}\ \overline{140}\ \overline{52}$

O. The ever-youthful Stignani

$\overline{66}\ \overline{122}\ \overline{189}$

P. Offenbach's 'Mann ohne Schatten'

$\overline{85}\ \overline{132}\ \overline{154}\ \overline{94}\ \overline{20}\ \overline{208}\ \overline{71}\ \overline{200}$

Q. They adorn the Cuvilliés Theatre (Ital.)

$\overline{134}\ \overline{166}\ \overline{6}\ \overline{35}\ \overline{75}$

R. She often responded to Melchior's 'Winterstürme' (2 words)

$\overline{180}\ \overline{12}\ \overline{135}\ \overline{224}\ \overline{21}$

$\overline{95}\ \overline{32}\ \overline{81}\ \overline{215}\ \overline{199}\ \overline{193}\ \overline{152}$

S. He takes Arabella for a sleigh ride

$\overline{34}\ \overline{204}\ \overline{163}\ \overline{87}\ \overline{46}\ \overline{187}$

T. Victor wrote operas on Hamlin's piper and Säkkingen's trumpeter

$\overline{10}\ \overline{138}\ \overline{191}\ \overline{181}\ \overline{69}\ \overline{129}\ \overline{110}$

U. Olin or Edward, Texaco quizmaster

$\overline{107}\ \overline{126}\ \overline{25}\ \overline{31}\ \overline{124}\ \overline{202}$

V. 'Hence away,' Mascagni heroine

$\overline{90}\ \overline{8}\ \overline{144}\ \overline{182}$

W. Gaetano wrote more than sixty operas in twenty-five years

$\overline{168}\ \overline{183}\ \overline{22}\ \overline{103}\ \overline{120}\ \overline{156}\ \overline{13}\ \overline{37}\ \overline{127}$

X. Italian countertenors: ____ *naturali*

$\overline{201}\ \overline{123}\ \overline{161}\ \overline{78}$

Y. Elisabeth often sang in z

$\overline{137}\ \overline{141}\ \overline{64}\ \overline{38}\ \overline{172}\ \overline{43}\ \overline{196}\ \overline{61}$

Z. Wagner's 1861 Paris fiasco

$\overline{139}\ \overline{58}\ \overline{62}\ \overline{184}\ \overline{99}\ \overline{48}\ \overline{218}\ \overline{97}\ \overline{53}\ \overline{190}$

a. Wilder town Bing wanted Copland to make into an opera

$\overline{112}\ \overline{186}\ \overline{44}$

b. Alberto disappointed 1890 Met subscribers with his *Asrael*

$\overline{160}\ \overline{54}\ \overline{16}\ \overline{104}\ \overline{128}\ \overline{108}\ \overline{158}\ \overline{80}\ \overline{150}\ \overline{84}$

c. Eugene conducted Bing's Met *Fledermaus*

$\overline{159}\ \overline{2}\ \overline{33}\ \overline{133}\ \overline{170}\ \overline{171}\ \overline{195}$

d. Luciano earned Met spurs with nine high Cs
    in *Fille* aria

    — — — — — — — — —
    212 73 198 27 174 131 117 113 179

e. Wotan gave one away for Fricka

    — — —
    106 70 142

f. Giovanni Battista surpassed all tenors in
    Bellini's day

    — — — — — —
    51 136 45 119 68 56

g. Aristocratic offstage presence in *Tosca*

    — — — — — — — — —
    76 153 49 88 125 30 79 114 60

The German Composer and
the American Soldier

Answers to the DEFINITIONS should be entered in the WORDS column and then transferred, letter by letter, to the appropriate squares in the GRID, where a quotation will gradually begin to form. Work back and forth between GRID and WORDS. When the puzzle is solved, the initial letters in the WORDS column will spell out the author and title of the book from which the quotation is taken. 'So, seid ihr fertig?' As Arabella says to Zdenka, 'Komm!'

1B	2Y	3O	4C	5W		6R	7O	8P		9D	10T	11X	12R	13N	14A	15H	16Q		17B	18Y
19B	20O	21P	22G		23R	24C	25W		26V	27J	28D	29I	30A	31B	32R	33H		34O	35C	
36T		37J	38N	39X	40V	41L	42O	43K		44P	45R	46B	47A	48Q	49N	50H		51O	52W	53F
54A	55C	56L	57R		58P	59O	60N	61U	62D	63M	64J		65S	66P		67G	68O	69T		70C
71S	72N	73D	74P	75R	76I	77E	78W	79X		80N	81O		82J	83R	84I		85B	86K	87M	88X
	89F		90P	91O		92W	93B	94R		95P	96U	97G	98C	99O	100S	101K	102R		103E	104J
	105H	106W	107L		108A	109J	110C	111R	112O	113C	114I	115Y	116F	117B	118M	119P	120D		121P	122Y
	123X	124W	125I	126V		127O	128W	129R		130B	131R	132Q		133A	134X	135O	136V	137W	138U	139Q
140N		141H	142R	143J	144X		145A	146O	147V	148Y		149F	150P		151H	152R	153X	154J	155T	
156W	157Y		158D	159A	160R	161P		162F		163P	164V	165K	166S		167O	168R		169P	170H	171M
172W	173U	174B	175F	176A	177J		178Y	179R	180V	181U	182W	183Q	184P		185X	186I	187Y		188R	189G
190L		191O	192T	193V	194N	195P		196B	197Q		198O	199H	200I		201A	202U	203B	204Y	205P	206C
207O																				

DEFINITIONS

A. Three first words of *Der Rosenkavalier*

B. Three spoken words in *Die Frau ohne Schatten*

C. Tenor role in *Daphne*

D. Tenor role in *Intermezzo*

E. Queen replaced by Semele in *Die Liebe der Danaë*

F. Soprano role in P

G. Subject matter preferred by O

H. Baritone role in *Arabella*

I. Strauss role created by Jeritza in 1912

J. What LaRoche did during Flamand's sextet (2 words)

WORDS

A. 201 14 176 47 159 145 54 108 133 30

B. 203 1 196 85 31 117 46 19 174 17 93 130

C. 4 206 55 113 24 98 70 35 110

D. 62 73 9 158 28 120

E. 77 103

F. 116 89 175 149 53 162

G. 97 22 67 189

H. 151 199 170 105 50 33 141 15

I. 114 76 125 186 200 29 84

J. 154 82 177 64 143 27 109 37 104

K. The Aegisth of AD 54–68

$\overline{43}\ \overline{101}\ \overline{165}\ \overline{86}$

L. Octavian's name for the Marschallin

$\overline{107}\ \overline{190}\ \overline{56}\ \overline{41}$

M. *Capriccio* Countess's last scene: ____ *Liebe schlägt mir entgegen*

$\overline{118}\ \overline{171}\ \overline{87}\ \overline{63}$

N. Pants role in *Ariadne auf Naxos*

$\overline{13}\ \overline{80}\ \overline{60}\ \overline{72}\ \overline{38}\ \overline{140}\ \overline{49}\ \overline{194}$

O. Strauss's librettist from 1909 to 1933

$\overline{198}\ \overline{3}\ \overline{42}\ \overline{167}\ \overline{20}\ \overline{191}\ \overline{112}$

$\overline{68}\ \overline{99}\ \overline{81}\ \overline{91}\ \overline{127}\ \overline{207}\ \overline{7}\ \overline{51}$

$\overline{34}\ \overline{146}\ \overline{59}\ \overline{135}$

P. 1928 Strauss opera (with *Die*)

$\overline{195}\ \overline{21}\ \overline{58}\ \overline{8}\ \overline{163}\ \overline{205}\ \overline{169}\ \overline{44}\ \overline{95}\ \overline{121}\ \overline{150}$

$\overline{161}\ \overline{119}\ \overline{74}\ \overline{184}\ \overline{66}\ \overline{90}$

Q. Fritz who conducted Dresden premiere of R

$\overline{139}\ \overline{197}\ \overline{48}\ \overline{16}\ \overline{132}\ \overline{183}$

R. 1919 Strauss opera

$\overline{129}\ \overline{12}\ \overline{152}\ \overline{168}\ \overline{102}\ \overline{6}\ \overline{179}\ \overline{45}\ \overline{131}\ \overline{83}\ \overline{111}$

$\overline{57}\ \overline{160}\ \overline{23}\ \overline{75}\ \overline{188}\ \overline{32}\ \overline{94}\ \overline{142}$

S. Fritz, the first 'Italian Singer'

$\overline{100}\ \overline{65}\ \overline{71}\ \overline{166}$

T. Tenor role in *Capriccio*

$\overline{155}\ \overline{36}\ \overline{10}\ \overline{192}\ \overline{69}$

U. Baritone role in *Intermezzo*

$\overline{202}\ \overline{96}\ \overline{61}\ \overline{138}\ \overline{173}\ \overline{181}$

V. Mezzo role in *Arabella*

$\overline{164}\ \overline{126}\ \overline{193}\ \overline{180}\ \overline{147}\ \overline{26}\ \overline{136}\ \overline{40}$

W. Country where the 'Symphonic Fragment' from *Josephslegende* premiered

$\overline{182}\ \overline{128}\ \overline{137}\ \overline{52}\ \overline{172}\ \overline{5}$

$\overline{156}\ \overline{78}\ \overline{124}\ \overline{92}\ \overline{106}\ \overline{25}$

X. Hans who supplied the sonnet in *Capriccio*

$\overline{11}\ \overline{144}\ \overline{153}\ \overline{39}\ \overline{134}\ \overline{185}\ \overline{123}\ \overline{88}\ \overline{79}$

Y. Appropriate marking for Salome's 'Er ist schrecklich!' (2 words, Ital.)

$\overline{187}\ \overline{18}\ \overline{204}\ \overline{148}\ \overline{157}\ \overline{115}\ \overline{2}\ \overline{178}\ \overline{122}$

Britten Waives the Rules

Answers to the DEFINITIONS should be entered in the WORDS column and then transferred, letter by letter, to the appropriate squares in the GRID, where a quotation will gradually begin to form. Work back and forth from GRID to WORDS. When the puzzle is solved, the initial letters in the WORDS column will spell out the author and title of the book from which the quotation is taken. So ship ahoy or, as the sailors' chantey has it in *Billy Budd*, 'O heave away, heave!'

1E	2H	3D	4O	5B	6A	7F	8S		9C	10K	11N	12F		13N	14M	15R	16C		17H	18B	19C		20C
21S		22O	23W	24M		25L	26H	27X	28R	29Y	30X		31Q	32D	33Q	34M	35L		36U	37X	38V	39W	40T
	41D	42W	43I	44C	45K	46a		47B	48F	49J	50G		51V	52L	53M	54N	55C		56G	57K	58A	59V	
60W	61Q		62W	63Y		64U	65Y	66D	67K	68W	69R	70C	71T		72S	73E		74C	75O	76H	77X	78T	79S
80a		81H	82E		83L		84D	85X	86C	87S	88B	89J	90Q		91W	92M	93H	94C		95O	96Q	97Y	98K
99M	100D	101R	102L	103B		104J	105X	106C	107R		108A		109H	110F	111a	112C		113E	114N	115Y	116I		117C
118H		119F	120B	121M		122C	123O	124K	125R	126Q	127D	128I		129R	130a		131Q	132N	133C	134X	135F	136X	137R
138D		139N	140V	141Z	142L	143Y	144C	145a		146R	147H		148H	149L	150Z		151H	152S	153W	154B	155X	156I	157Z
158X		159V	160H		161D		162E	163K	164L	165G		166Y	167P		168S	169W	170G	171X	172R		173C	174I	175Q
176O		177W		178K	179Y	180X		181N	182M		183G	184a	185D		186E	187a	188M	189F		190R	191B		192a
193F	194B		195O	196D	197A		198R	199T	200C	201X		202a	203K		204Y	205C	206M		207S	208T	209H		210L
211A	212D	213Q		214K	215H	216O	217M		218B	219D		220Y	221M		222D	223P	224a	225U		226H	227T	228Q
229U	230Z	231C		232D	233Q		234H	235E	236L	237B	238O	239T	240G		241R	242N	243W	244X		245T		246C	247H
248F	249R		250E	251a		252B	253R																

DEFINITIONS

A. W.H., Britten's first librettist

B. Challenge for Wechsler in *Peter Grimes*; reverse of seeing a light? (3 words)

C. Britten opera, 1960 (4 words)

D. Composer in *Let's Make an Opera!*

E. Fisherman and Methodist in *Peter Grimes*

F. Essex sings two to Elizabeth in T (2 words)

G. Aschenbach: 'Does beauty lead to wisdom, Paedrus? ____ ____ through the senses.'

WORDS

___ ___ ___ ___ ___
108 211 197 6 58

___ ___ ___ ___ ___ ___ ___ ___
88 218 103 120 5 252 191 194

___ ___ ___ ___
18 47 154 237

___ ___ ___ ___ ___ ___ ___ ___ ___ ___
70 133 20 112 55 205 122 173 16 144

___ ___ ___ ___ ___ ___
19 117 86 9 106 200

___ ___ ___ ___ ___
231 44 94 74 246

___ ___ ___ ___ ___ ___
196 32 84 222 185 100

___ ___ ___ ___ ___ ___ ___ ___ ___
212 66 161 41 219 3 127 138 232

___ ___ ___ ___ ___ ___ ___ ___
186 82 113 1 250 162 73 235

___ ___ ___ ___ ___ ___ ___ ___ ___
189 48 119 12 248 110 7 193 135

___ ___ ___ ___ ___ ___
240 50 165 56 170 183

H. Britten opera, 1954 (5 words)

<u> </u> <u> </u> <u> </u> <u> </u> <u> </u> <u> </u> <u> </u> <u> </u> <u> </u>
209 226 26 160 234 17 118 215 93

<u> </u> <u> </u> <u> </u> <u> </u> <u> </u> <u> </u> <u> </u> <u> </u>
81 76 147 151 109 2 247 148

I. Challenge for Vickers in Peter Grimes's 'I'll marry Ellen' (2 words)

116 43 128 156 174

J. Condition of John's neck in Act 2 of *Peter Grimes*

49 89 104

K. Conductor, Met premiere of *Peter Grimes*

57 214 98 45 178 10 163 203 67 124

L. Guy de ____, wrote short-story source of *Albert Herring*

210 52 236 25 149 35 164 83 102 142

M. Mrs Sedley: 'Murder most foul it is ____ ____ ____ ____.'

217 121 24 188 221 53 182 92 99 34

14 206

N. Last two words in H (Lat.)

139 242 54 132 11 114 13 181

O. Retired skipper in *Peter Grimes*

95 195 238 22 4 216 123 75 176

P. Conductor, premiere of *The Rape of Lucretia* (init.)

167 223

Q. Under protest, he gives his name as Joseph Higgins (2 words)

90 233 131

31 213 126 61 175 96 33 228

R. Owen: '____ ____ ____ ____ you all.'

137 190 241 15 129 125 69 249 107

28 172 198 101 253 146

S. One of the royal palaces in T

207 152 21 79 8 87 168 72

T. Britten opera, 1953

40 239 208 78 227 245 71 199

U. Big Blue Ox that A deliberately left out of *Paul Bunyan*

229 36 64 225

V. First auxiliary seats at Snape Maltings? (2 words)

51 38 59 140 159

W. First five words in *Billy Budd*

23 42 153 177 62 169 91 243

68 60 39

X. Britten opera, 1949 (3 words)

$\overline{136}$ $\overline{201}$ $\overline{77}$ $\overline{37}$ $\overline{105}$ $\overline{158}$ $\overline{27}$ $\overline{171}$ $\overline{244}$

$\overline{30}$ $\overline{155}$ $\overline{85}$ $\overline{134}$ $\overline{180}$

Y. George Crabbe poem, source of *Peter Grimes* (2 words)

$\overline{115}$ $\overline{166}$ $\overline{143}$ $\overline{204}$ $\overline{65}$ $\overline{29}$ $\overline{63}$ $\overline{179}$ $\overline{97}$ $\overline{220}$

Z. Part of Suffolk in which *Albert Herring* is set

$\overline{230}$ $\overline{157}$ $\overline{150}$ $\overline{141}$

a. Britten opera, 1958 (2 words)

$\overline{130}$ $\overline{187}$ $\overline{46}$ $\overline{192}$ $\overline{145}$

$\overline{251}$ $\overline{111}$ $\overline{202}$ $\overline{80}$ $\overline{224}$ $\overline{184}$

The Twentieth-Century Composer
Speaks

Answers to the DEFINITIONS should be entered in the WORDS column and then transferred, letter by letter, to the appropriate squares in the GRID, where a quotation will gradually begin to form. Work back and forth between GRID and WORDS. When the puzzle is solved, the initial letters in the WORDS column will spell out the author and title of the book from which the quotation is taken. So take courage! As Gertrude Stein observed to Virgil Thomson, 'It is easy to be right.'

1H		2I	3W		4X		5Q	6Y	7A	8D	9W	10B	11H	12C		13Q	14I	15L	16G		17W	18M	
19C	20Z	21R	22X	23V	24W	25Y		26Y	27H	28W		29G	30C	31D	32N	33Q	34G	35W	36J		37H	38B	39E
40O	41M	42X		43G	44R	45Q		46K	47T	48C	49D	50X	51U	52G		53M	54N	55I	56D	57Y		58G	59Z
60X	61H		62I	63W	64L		65C	66Q	67N		68W	69H	70Z	71S	72I	73H	74Y	75X		76Q	77W	78M	79Z
	80K	81T		82W	83Y	84B	85G	86H	87A		88F	89M		90E	91R	92Z	93C	94P	95G	96X	97Q		98J
99H	100W	101D	102X	103Q	104M	105G	106W		107H	108B	109K		110Y		111W	112H	113S	114Q		115G	116R	117Q	118Y
119W	120P	121Y	122D	123X	124Q	125J		126W		127T	128U	129J	130C	131M	132F	133L	134Q		135Y	136D	137I	138B	139H
140X		141H	142M	143O	144D		145C	146S	147Y	148A	149W	150K	151Q		152G	153V	154Z		155Y	156W	157M		158V
159X	160D	161O	162R	163Q	164G		165C	166W		167S	168J		169X	170B	171A	172W	173T	174Q	175I	176G	177O	178N	179C
	180W	181Y	182P		183F	184W	185Z	186G	187X	188M	189D		190W	191C	192Y	193H	194L	195C	196X	197Q		198B	199O
	200T	201W	202P		203X	204Q	205I	206Y	207S	208H	209W		210M	211E		212H	213Q	214J	215Z	216Y		217G	218K
219A	220W	221S	222X		223H	224Y	225Q	226W	227U		228L	229V	230A	231N	232J	233Q	234D	235W	236F	237R	238X		239I
240W	241E	242Y	243X	244H		245Z	246I	247U		248W	249C	250Q	251G	252W		253K	254M		255I	256W	257X	

DEFINITIONS

A. King Fisher's clairvoyant (with z)

B. Virgil, composer of *Lord Byron*

C. Painterly style of *Pelléas*

D. Fourth sea interlude in *Peter Grimes*

E. Feline Lord in *The English Cat*

F. Fischer or Cooper

G. Time span for the entries in this puzzle (2 words)

H. Farcical Rota opus (4 words, Eng.)

WORDS

A. <u>7</u> <u>148</u> <u>87</u> <u>171</u> <u>230</u> <u>219</u>

B. <u>198</u> <u>138</u> <u>38</u> <u>170</u> <u>10</u> <u>84</u> <u>108</u>

C. <u>249</u> <u>30</u> <u>145</u> <u>12</u> <u>191</u> <u>130</u> <u>19</u> <u>195</u> <u>165</u> <u>179</u>
<u>65</u> <u>93</u> <u>48</u>

D. <u>8</u> <u>160</u> <u>49</u> <u>144</u> <u>31</u> <u>101</u> <u>122</u> <u>189</u>
<u>56</u> <u>136</u> <u>234</u>

E. <u>90</u> <u>39</u> <u>241</u> <u>211</u>

F. <u>236</u> <u>88</u> <u>132</u> <u>183</u>

G. <u>16</u> <u>58</u> <u>251</u> <u>95</u> <u>176</u> <u>29</u> <u>217</u> <u>43</u> <u>152</u>
<u>115</u> <u>52</u> <u>34</u> <u>186</u> <u>85</u> <u>105</u> <u>164</u>

H. <u>212</u> <u>61</u> <u>11</u> <u>1</u> <u>208</u> <u>99</u> <u>73</u> <u>139</u> <u>193</u> <u>86</u>
<u>37</u> <u>141</u> <u>69</u> <u>107</u> <u>223</u> <u>27</u> <u>112</u> <u>244</u>

I. Source for *Savitri* and Brook's Brooklyn marathon

$\overline{255}$ $\overline{205}$ $\overline{14}$ $\overline{2}$ $\overline{72}$ $\overline{246}$ $\overline{62}$

$\overline{55}$ $\overline{175}$ $\overline{137}$ $\overline{239}$

J. Source for *Pénélope* and Bungert's bungled Rhine cycle

$\overline{214}$ $\overline{232}$ $\overline{125}$ $\overline{36}$ $\overline{98}$ $\overline{129}$ $\overline{168}$

K. It works its magic in *Koanga*

$\overline{218}$ $\overline{46}$ $\overline{150}$ $\overline{109}$ $\overline{80}$ $\overline{253}$

L. Tajo or Montemezzi

$\overline{228}$ $\overline{194}$ $\overline{15}$ $\overline{64}$ $\overline{133}$

M. Timely Hindemith opus (4 words, Eng.)

$\overline{188}$ $\overline{78}$ $\overline{53}$ $\overline{18}$ $\overline{210}$ $\overline{254}$ $\overline{131}$ $\overline{142}$ $\overline{157}$

$\overline{41}$ $\overline{104}$ $\overline{89}$

N. Mother in *The Rake's Progress*

$\overline{32}$ $\overline{178}$ $\overline{54}$ $\overline{67}$ $\overline{231}$

O. Setting for Reimann's *Troades*

$\overline{177}$ $\overline{161}$ $\overline{143}$ $\overline{199}$ $\overline{40}$

P. Britten fludde survivor

$\overline{120}$ $\overline{94}$ $\overline{182}$ $\overline{202}$

Q. Pastoral Janáček opus (4 words, Eng.)

$\overline{163}$ $\overline{213}$ $\overline{45}$ $\overline{5}$ $\overline{103}$ $\overline{174}$ $\overline{117}$ $\overline{225}$ $\overline{197}$ $\overline{76}$

$\overline{124}$ $\overline{233}$ $\overline{13}$ $\overline{66}$ $\overline{97}$ $\overline{204}$

$\overline{250}$ $\overline{33}$ $\overline{151}$ $\overline{114}$ $\overline{134}$

R. Helen sang in the Met's only broadcast *Rondine*

$\overline{116}$ $\overline{237}$ $\overline{44}$ $\overline{91}$ $\overline{162}$ $\overline{21}$

S. Naval battle in Barber's *Antony and Cleopatra*

$\overline{146}$ $\overline{113}$ $\overline{221}$ $\overline{207}$ $\overline{71}$ $\overline{167}$

T. Bly spirit in *Turn of the Screw*

$\overline{127}$ $\overline{47}$ $\overline{173}$ $\overline{81}$ $\overline{200}$

U. Hermann sang in the Met's first *Wozzeck*

$\overline{128}$ $\overline{227}$ $\overline{51}$ $\overline{247}$

V. Calaf's name, according to Turandot (Ital.)

$\overline{153}$ $\overline{229}$ $\overline{23}$ $\overline{158}$

W. Trenchant Weill opus (8 words, Eng.), with 'The'

$\overline{190}$ $\overline{17}$ $\overline{252}$ $\overline{35}$ $\overline{184}$ $\overline{100}$ $\overline{149}$

$\overline{111}$ $\overline{180}$ $\overline{63}$ $\overline{248}$ $\overline{28}$ $\overline{166}$ $\overline{68}$ $\overline{156}$ $\overline{256}$

$\overline{226}$ $\overline{119}$ $\overline{235}$ $\overline{209}$ $\overline{9}$ $\overline{240}$

$\overline{3}$ $\overline{126}$ $\overline{201}$ $\overline{82}$ $\overline{172}$ $\overline{77}$ $\overline{220}$ $\overline{24}$ $\overline{106}$

X. Song sung by Sportin' Life (4 words, Eng.)

$\overline{187}$ $\overline{102}$ $\overline{4}$ $\overline{50}$ $\overline{257}$ $\overline{60}$ $\overline{140}$ $\overline{22}$ $\overline{243}$ $\overline{159}$

$\overline{75}$ $\overline{222}$ $\overline{96}$ $\overline{203}$ $\overline{169}$ $\overline{123}$ $\overline{238}$ $\overline{42}$ $\overline{196}$

Y. Dance tune from *Vanessa* (4 words, Eng.)

<u>121</u> <u>181</u> <u>57</u> <u>25</u> <u>83</u> <u>118</u> <u>224</u> <u>242</u>

<u>26</u> <u>110</u> <u>206</u> <u>192</u> <u>6</u> <u>135</u> <u>155</u> <u>147</u> <u>216</u> <u>74</u>

Z. Completes A

<u>215</u> <u>20</u> <u>154</u> <u>70</u> <u>185</u> <u>245</u> <u>92</u> <u>59</u> <u>79</u>

The Old and the New

Answers to the DEFINITIONS should be entered in the WORDS column, and then transferred, letter by letter, to the appropriate squares in the GRID, where a quotation will gradually begin to form. Work back and forth from GRID to WORDS. When the puzzle is solved, the initial letters in the WORDS column will spell out the author and title of the book from which the quotation is taken. As Faust says when changed from old to new, 'En route!'

1A	2P	3R	4O	5I		6Q	7C	8X	9H	10B		11Y	12M		13L	14F	15J	16D		17F	18L	19O	20V
	21R	22X	23B	24M	25Z	26S	27U		28T	29V	30N	31G		32b	33Y	34M	35F	36b	37Z		38G	39R	40a
41V	42b		43Z	44T	45W		46b	47J		48F	49Q	50S		51X	52X	53X	54X	55X	56Z		57L	58O	59M
60Z	61U	62b	63H	64B		65X	66b	67G	68D	69D	70F	71A		72G	73H	74b	75X		76H	77Q	78b		79F
80M	81G	82J	83L	84U	85E	86Y	87C		88E	89B	90G	91O	92C		93A	94b	95H	96b	97X	98D	99T	100F	101O
102L		103B		104A	105D	106Y	107G	108N	109Q	110K		111B	112Z	113L	114Z	115R	116H	117B	118Z	119N		120M	121O
122P	123F	124A	125F	126T	127L		128Z	129D		130M	131b	132V	133O	134V	135M	136T	137K		138G	139L	140I		141A
142O	143Y	144M	145Y	146F	147R	148Z	149L	150F	151U	152Z		153a	154T	155B	156X	157R		158V	159F	160C		161P	162W
163b	164O	165S		166R	167P	168b	169V	170A		171F	172X	173S		174E	175B		176M		177R	178F	179Y	180C	181b
182M	183H	184B		185b	186V		187Y	188M	189C	190S	191V	192O		193b	194F	195Y	196L	197X	198U		199b	200L	201A
	202N	203S	204U	205b	206H	207b	208J	209D	210Z	211W	212B		213P	214F		215E	216b	217J		218b	219X	220C	221T
222W	223a	224F	225I		226H	227B	228L	229F		230H	231G	232E	233V	234H	235a	236D	237S	238Y		239K	240U	241I	
242L	243D	244V	245Q	246G	247O	248Y		249I	250L	251Y	252D	253P	254K	255T	256S	257G	258D	259W	260T	261H	262J

DEFINITIONS

A. Picturesque Granados opera

‾124 ‾1 ‾71 ‾201 ‾141 ‾93 ‾170 ‾104

B. Triskaidekaphobic English title for Schoenberg opera (3 words)

‾23 ‾227 ‾212 ‾111 ‾117 ‾103 ‾184 ‾10

‾155 ‾64 ‾89 ‾175

C. Joseph, an addled spectator at Handel opera

‾87 ‾160 ‾92 ‾180 ‾189 ‾7 ‾220

D. Katia, a Karajan Turandot

‾209 ‾69 ‾252 ‾243 ‾105 ‾98 ‾129 ‾16 ‾258 ‾68 ‾236

E. Adjective for Menotti's Toby or Auber's Fenella

‾215 ‾232 ‾88 ‾174 ‾85

F. Opening G & S chorus, almost translates Oscar's 'Saper vorreste' (6 words)

‾100 ‾214 ‾224 ‾14 ‾123 ‾48 ‾194 ‾159 ‾70

‾229 ‾178 ‾35 ‾146 ‾79 ‾17 ‾171 ‾125 ‾150

G. Porter tune done à la Berlin (3 words)

‾246 ‾67 ‾81 ‾138 ‾72 ‾90 ‾31 ‾38

‾231 ‾257 ‾107

H. Michael conducted first U.S. three-act Lulu (2 words)

‾76 ‾261 ‾9 ‾230 ‾206 ‾95

‾234 ‾73 ‾183 ‾226 ‾63 ‾116

WORDS

I. Puccini's Angelica provides herbs to ease their sting

$\overline{241}\ \overline{5}\ \overline{225}\ \overline{249}\ \overline{140}$

J. Biblical Handel oratorio

$\overline{208}\ \overline{262}\ \overline{47}\ \overline{82}\ \overline{217}\ \overline{15}$

K. Unlikely subject of Shostakovich opera

$\overline{239}\ \overline{254}\ \overline{110}\ \overline{137}$

L. River immortalized in Kern operetta (2 words)

$\overline{102}\ \overline{200}\ \overline{83}\ \overline{13}\ \overline{149}\ \overline{250}\ \overline{127}\ \overline{18}\ \overline{228}$

$\overline{242}\ \overline{196}\ \overline{113}\ \overline{57}\ \overline{139}$

M. Love duet in Handel's *Rodelinda* (2 words, Ital.)

$\overline{130}\ \overline{12}\ \overline{120}\ \overline{176}\ \overline{188}\ \overline{24}\ \overline{80}\ \overline{135}\ \overline{59}$

$\overline{144}\ \overline{182}\ \overline{34}$

N. Miss Moser or a source for the *Ring*

$\overline{108}\ \overline{202}\ \overline{119}\ \overline{30}$

O. Heated Robert Ward opera (2 words)

$\overline{19}\ \overline{121}\ \overline{58}\ \overline{247}\ \overline{4}\ \overline{142}\ \overline{101}\ \overline{133}$

$\overline{192}\ \overline{91}\ \overline{164}$

P. Last two words of *Wozzeck* (Eng.)

$\overline{161}\ \overline{122}\ \overline{167}\ \overline{253}\ \overline{213}\ \overline{2}$

Q. Friedrich completed *Lulu's* Act 3

$\overline{6}\ \overline{245}\ \overline{109}\ \overline{77}\ \overline{49}$

R. Quick coffee at Biffi's before La Scala

$\overline{3}\ \overline{157}\ \overline{177}\ \overline{39}\ \overline{115}\ \overline{21}\ \overline{147}\ \overline{166}$

S. Compatriots Christine and Birgit

$\overline{256}\ \overline{203}\ \overline{26}\ \overline{165}\ \overline{50}\ \overline{190}\ \overline{237}\ \overline{173}$

T. Atmospheric Korngold opera, *Die* ____ ____ (2 words)

$\overline{126}\ \overline{44}\ \overline{221}\ \overline{154}\ \overline{260}\ \overline{28}\ \overline{255}\ \overline{99}\ \overline{136}$

U. Title character in operas by Monteverdi and Dallapiccola (Eng.)

$\overline{151}\ \overline{61}\ \overline{198}\ \overline{27}\ \overline{84}\ \overline{240}\ \overline{204}$

V. Genial producer of Met broadcast intermissions 1981–93

$\overline{191}\ \overline{244}\ \overline{134}\ \overline{20}\ \overline{158}\ \overline{233}\ \overline{132}$

$\overline{41}\ \overline{186}\ \overline{29}\ \overline{169}$

W. Porter tune: '____ the Top'

$\overline{259}\ \overline{162}\ \overline{222}\ \overline{45}\ \overline{211}$

X. Founded by Irene and Sherwin Sloan (2 words)

$\overline{51}\ \overline{52}\ \overline{53}\ \overline{54}\ \overline{55}$

$\overline{65}\ \overline{8}\ \overline{172}\ \overline{97}\ \overline{75}\ \overline{219}\ \overline{156}\ \overline{197}\ \overline{22}$

Y. Gershwin's self-styled 'folk opera' (3 words)

$\overline{33}\ \overline{145}\ \overline{86}\ \overline{238}\ \overline{251}\ \overline{187}\ \overline{106}\ \overline{11}$

$\overline{143}\ \overline{248}\ \overline{179}\ \overline{195}$

z. *The ____ ____ Mr Brouček* (2 words)

‾‾ ‾‾ ‾‾ ‾‾ ‾‾ ‾‾ ‾‾ ‾‾ ‾‾ ‾‾
118 112 148 60 114 56 210 25 37 152

‾‾ ‾‾
128 43

a. Torsten, a twentieth-century Titan

‾‾ ‾‾ ‾‾ ‾‾
223 40 235 153

b. Arlen/Mercer tune associated with Lawrence Tibbett (3 words)

‾‾ ‾‾ ‾‾ ‾‾ ‾‾ ‾‾ ‾‾ ‾‾ ‾‾ ‾‾
74 205 218 36 131 199 66 42 181 168

‾‾ ‾‾ ‾‾
96 216 78

‾‾ ‾‾ ‾‾ ‾‾ ‾‾ ‾‾ ‾‾ ‾‾
163 94 32 62 185 46 207 193

ACT V

Crosswords

Opera Cruise

Dawn and night on the sea. Rainbows. Many languages. Initialed luggage destined for native states. Operatic personalities on board. Puns, anagrams, and French opera choruses. Overheard bits of conversation from characters in costume. That's our crossword opera cruise. Care to come aboard? As the Captain says to the would-be cabin boy in *Manon Lescaut*, 'V'affrettate!'

ACROSS

1. *Attila* crossed it in 1850; you can use canoe
10. *Samson* chorus: 'Nous avons _____ nos cités renversées'
11. U.S. opera stars sang here during WWII
12. High-flying Galli-Gurci encore: '_____ here the gentle lark'
13. They appear *en ciel* at the end of operas by Wagner and Honegger
15. Native state (abbrev.) for Helen Donath (Corpus Christi) and Thomas Stewart (San Saba)
16. Use wand to make *Ring* interlude appear
18. *Hoffmann* chorus: '_____ sommes les amis des hommes'
19. She's supposed to lead on a swan in *Tannhäuser*
20. Almost sheer with the opening chord, she has the first word in *Arabella*
21. Count Horn's U.S. alias
23. Critic unsurpassed to ye Verdians
25. The *Ring*'s gold in Rennes
26. Falke's favourite pronoun

27. It introduces *Corsaro* and *Campiello*
29. Stafford Deane or Suzanne Danco
30. He didn't want to leave the poor girl flatless
31. Martha Mödl or Michael Myers
33. Sarah Caldwell or Schuyler Chapin
34. Elisabeth Grümmer, for example
35. *Carmen* chorus: 'Pour loi, ____ volonté'
36. Find this advocate of *fuggir* in Adidas running shoes
39. Mikado: '____ by Bach interwoven with Spohr and Beethoven'
41. Shepherd: 'Öd und leer das ____'
43. Apostrophized in *Faust, Hoffmann, Troyens* duets
44. Gustav III threw one, fatally
45. 41 down loses letter, ends up nameless and abbreviated
46. Arturo: '____ ____, o cara'
48. Dr Bartolo: 'O ciel, che ____!'
50. Hometown state (abbrev.) for Nelson Eddy (Providence) and Eileen Farrell (Woonsocket)
51. Familiar name for Miss Price
52. Ken Neate or Kent Nagano
53. *Aida* crossed it in 1872; you use Medean terrain

DOWN

1. Miss June of the ENO
2. Seascape artist or a dame we'd like to see return
3. Rossini prince with an eye for Russia
4. Akhnaten's son-in-law reproaches mildly
5. Ponchielli notary has poise
6. Tenor Jean or director John
7. Put this soldier in a gypsy den and he turns decadent
8. Berlin song, or Lulu's lover linked with Lalo locale
9. Opening word in arias by Calaf, Cenerentola, Cherubino
14. Miss Glade of the touring San Carlo
17. Miss Annie of *Oklahoma!* or part of *Beatrice* source
20. Verdi librettist Antonio, anagrammed his name to Tommaso Anoni
21. Rossini sultan leaves court to court in Naples
22. Roman soldier finds smile in Britten boy
24. Lucy of Lammermoor's beloved
26. It introduces *Rheingold* and *Liebesverbot*
28. Break this for good luck
32. 'Me? I keep the inn surrounded,' said this barmaid
35. She and Nelusko are look alikes

37. Two voices, not altogether loud
38. *Faust* chorus: '____ que la brise légère'
40. Disarranged French priest becomes German broommaker or English fisherman
41. Scramble Février's Vanna to get Massenet's Lescaut
42. Zerlina: '____ ____ speziale non lo sa far'
45. Break this too for good luck
46. Little John: 'I'll sing the praise of brown October ____'
47. Jupiter: 'Where ____ you walk'
49. Miss Murray of Covent Garden

Bell-Shaped Tones

Which composer might have boasted, 'I always cast a diva in bell-shaped tones'? Bellini, if he were in a punning and anagrammatic mood: not only did he compose 'Casta diva,' but three of the words in this boast (I ... in ... bell) go together to spell out his name. Such puns and anagrams are the main matter of the sixteen words ACROSS in this puzzle. The words DOWN are brief factual bits to ease your onward passage. So, as a bell-shaped diva sings in another Bellini opera, 'Vieni, vieni.'

ACROSS

1. Erich's music for stage & screen was amber waves of grain
6. Siegfried wishes he would shut up and just act the part
8. Peter had bell-shaped tones to spare
11. This Theophilus could disarm a Medusa
15. For Ferruccio, say 'si buon'
19. Jennie knew how to see the real Chicago
22. Critic naps, then uses kitchenware for snap judgment
24. Gounod homebody finds frat house a dud
29. Hellenized god poisoned atmosphere in *Idomeneo*
34. She could double-dare Wotan to read his runes

36. Venetian inquisitor revealed as evil
39. French opera hero served with short order of eggs
44. Handel seductress solfegges at the sandwich shop
48. Jupiter's disguise for visiting Richard Strauss maids
52. Jacopo thought opera ripe for inventing
53. Offenbach's Emil received no zeroes in school

DOWN

2. Song for Gounod's Sapho
3. Lohengrin: 'O Elsa! ____ ein Jahr an deiner Seite'
4. Agathe: '____ Mond auf seinem Pfad wohl lacht?'
5. Sachs: '____ Vogel, der heut' sang'
6. Big scene for Sutherland or Sills
7. Alma mater for 'Ol' Man River'?
8. Delius's Paradise Garden, e.g.
9. Wotan, 'Wala, erwach'! ____ langem Schlaf'
10. Norma: '____ io'
11. Fidès: '____, mon fils!'
12. Gioconda: 'Enzo adorato! Ah, come t'____'
13. Any singer needs a good one
14. Radamès: 'Un trono vicino al ____'
16. Nemorino: '____ furtiva lagrima'
17. Mikado: 'A series of masses and fugues and ____'
18. Figure attending Boito's Mephisto?
19. Roméo: 'Ah! lève-____, soleil'
20. Marguerite: 'Comme ____ demoiselle'
21. Org. for London Opera
22. *Higglety Pigglety* ____!
23. Roméo and Juliette: 'Le ciel reçoit ____ serments amoureux'
25. '____ here the gentle lark'
26. Enzo: 'Cielo e ____'
27. Org. for Weber's Max
28. Mimì: '____, mi chiamano Mimì'
30. Bird for Lady Macbeth
31. Renato: '____ tu, che macchiavi'
32. Holländer: '____ Frist ist um'
33. Japanese opera?
34. Tree for Wagner's 'Waldweben'?
35. This Met Doris was a dear
36. *Fennimore* ____ *Gerda*
37. Pinkerton: 'Ah! son ____'

38. Aida: 'Sul me, _____ padre mio'
40. Rodolfo takes Mimì's in Act 1
41. Sir Joseph: 'When I was a _____ I served a term'
42. Wrestling Bradford: '_____ an earth defiled'
43. Gounod's Mephisto: '_____ bien, docteur, que me veux-tu?'
45. Character in Penderecki's *Paradise Lost*
46. Mélisande: 'Je reste _____'
47. Wolfram: '_____ du im kühnem Sange'
49. Tippett break
50. Carmen: 'Chez mon _____ Lillas Pastia'
51. Carlo: '_____ de' verd'anni miei'

Aria Crossword

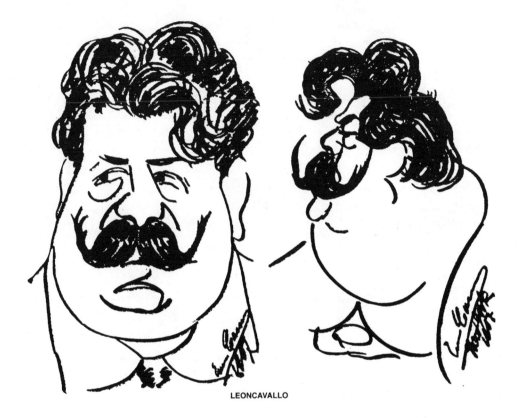

LEONCAVALLO

Our puzzle concerns itself solely with opera, from aria titles to truncated quotes, puns, anagrams, and multiple clues. Keep your languages handy. As the four Bohemians say, 'Andiam!'

ACROSS

1. ARIA: Verdi soprano takes last look in mirror (3 words)
14. Archibaldo and friends on evening in France
15. A lone town near Chautauqua festival
16. Wagner father to his son: 'Sei _____'
17. Plato dialogue, Euripides tragicomedy, electrically charged particle, Polish tenor Buzea
18. Manon to her *petit table*: 'Ah, pauvre _____'
19. First word of Grace Moore movie title
21. Enzo to the Adriatic: 'Cielo e _____'
22. ARIA: Gounod tenor gives way to lustful feelings (4 words)
26. London's popular-priced opera reverses 19 across
27. Our poet's rhetorical device, abounding in *Salome* text
31. When, Ernesto sings, nights are uncommonly lovely
35. ARIA: Rossini baritone asks for room (3 words)

36. Extra in *Der Freischütz* (Ger.); he published first guide to historic opera recordings (1898–1909)
37. Chicago bass, film Hans Sachs, and soundtrack Émile de Becque
38. Carmen Jones's José
41. ARIA: Puccini tenor falls in love at first sight (4 words)
51. What Lisa's and Fedora's card-playing lovers may be said to do
52. Hymns to him are sung in *Iris*, *Snegurochka*, and *Le coq d'or*
53. True identity of Henze's Junge Lord
54. What Tosca lived for, what the MGM lion roared for (Lat.)
55. Stage props in *Manon*, *Merry Mount*, and *Meistersinger*
57. Turiddu to his best friend: '____, quel vino!'
59. First bone to burn in *Muzio Scevola*?
60. ARIA: Wagner mezzo invokes outcast gods (2 words)

DOWN

1. Any of 1, 22, 35, 41, 60 across
2. Mood impending in *verismo* operas
3. Tenor Borgioli or stage director Yannopoulos
4. Frederic to the ladies' chorus: 'Oh, ____ there not one maiden breast'
5. Lakmé and Mallika sing modish barcarolle about it (Fr.)
6. Soprano Elizza or soprano Stevenson (both fl. 1910), or lady to whom Beethoven dedicated familiar *Albumblatt*
7. ____ *Prophète*
8. Verdi villain compelled to curse himself
9. Palindromatic Mozart or Puccini heroine
10. Virgil Thomson character (abbrev.)
11. Manrico to his soldiers: 'All'____'
12. Contemporary English tenor or subject of Donizetti aria
13. Possessive; accompanies Siegfried on his entry in Paris
18. Gilda to her father: 'Tutte le feste ____ tempio'
20. Stage prop for *Königskinder* (Ger.) or Eva to Sachs: '____ was, zu alt!'
23. Stage surname of famous soprano Inge von Guenther
24. Smetana's masterpiece (init.) or soprano who introduced 'Climb Ev'ry Mountain' (init.)
25. Florentine composer, cofounder of opera; Venetian librettist for Monteverdi; Genovese painter famed for his *Lute Player*
27. What wealthy New Yorker sometimes picks up for Met production
28. Otello to Desdemona: 'A te____, e piangi!'
29. His voyage is subject of opera by Dominick Argento
30. Turiddu gets his bitten
31. Operatic division; what opera singers are often said not to do

32. Will Cleo's brother (abbrev.) please turn over?
33. Mascagni friend sans 'Fr.'
34. Donna Elvira to the avenging deities: 'Per ____ pietà'
38. He gets a verse from Sporting Life
39. Cassandra to no listeners: '____ s'arrête. O dieux!'
40. Pogner to the masters: '____ ____in einzig Kind, zur Eh'!'
41. What Chim-Fen traffics in; what Rodgers's *Allegro* gentleman is
42. Gravebound Britten hero who faces family ghosts
43. It went as stage prop for Peter Hall's Met *Macbeth*
44. Ko-Ko to the gentleman of Japan: '____ some day it may happen'
45. Aida (or *Idomeneo*'s chorus) to the avenging deities: '____ pietà'
46. 'Rid____ ____liaccio'
47. Valentin to his Seigneur: 'Avant ____ quitter ces lieux'
48. It flavours the drinks quaffed by Johann and Schmidt
49. Composer of 'Sally in Our Alley' and the masque of Milton's *Comus*
50. River presided over by Prinzregententheater
56. Direction taken by Isolde's ship (abbrev.), or Mrs McCracken (init.)
58. Milanov's teacher (init.) or Ponselle's Adalgisa (init.)
59. *Solfeggio* start and finish; Verdi 'you' seen in mirror

La Triviata

If you can see how Thaïs could be taken for Siamese twins or how Wotan might wow them at NATO, if you can find Napoli in the middle of Anapolis, then you shouldn't have much trouble with the Lily puns and *Gloriana* grams in this puzzle. Some expertise with libretti and their languages will come in handy along the way. As the entire company sings at the end of *Figaro*, 'Corriam tutti!'

1	2	3		4	5		6		7	8		9	10	11
12				13					14			15		
16				17		18		19				20		
21					22							23		
24			25	26	27				28	29	30			
			31						32					
			33						34					
35	36	37							38			39	40	41
42					43		44					45		
46				47	48				49	50		51		
52				53					54			55		
56									57					

ACROSS

1. Could be a pants part for Elsie
7. Hat girl can brush off the fuzz or a fed
12. He's seen with Sam
13. Claggart: 'So may it ____'
14. Initials for *Zaza* composer
15. Miss Cio-Cio
16. Elsa seems to have it, especially
17. Robert's ram-horned father
20. Wagner cycle with lost eye
21. Cherubino: '____ che sapete'
22. Des Grieux: '____ voi, belle'
23. Surface for *Prophète* ballet
24. Vanessa expected another, alas!
28. Metathesize Catholic mission for Protestant retainer
31. Otello: '____ e per sempre addio'

32. Pelléas's entrance: 'Une lettre de mon ____ Marcellus'
33. Mme Lidoine (often): '____ filles'
34. Mélisande's entrance: 'Ne me touchez ____'
35. Find *bel canto* hero in a bottle
38. Reset nothing, it's sounding from all directions
42. Rhine's gold in Orvieto
43. 'I Menotti boy,' said Martin over this
45. Zerbinetta: '____ ein Gott kam jeder gegangen'
46. Short street in Bayreuth
47. 'Are you the law around here?' he asked his critics
51. Janáček case
52. One of 'the Five,' he wrote ten operas
53. David: '____ Jordan Sankt'
54. Ulrica: '____ dell'abisso'
55. Knock the Hel out of Demetrius's sweetheart
56. Add E to boost confidence of Rossini madman
57. Euryanthe's beau almost makes a buck

DOWN

1. Reinvest a Spontini goddess as Janáček cad
2. Adriana: '____ ____ l'umile ancella'
3. Amneris: '____ razza! anatema su voi!'
4. End of *Peter Grimes*: 'It rolls in ____ yet terrible and deep'
5. *Quarterly* quizzer
6. Where Mottl was acclaimed in opera
7. Pizzetti's Gherardo
8. Tree for Tippett's Mel
9. Thomas dropped him from *Hamlet, je crois*
10. Jack would crane a neck, all right
11. Who would glean Renata saw Heinrich as this?
18. Tauber monogram
19. Arié monogram
25. Find *Aida* scene in bottom
26. Find cookie in 1607 opera
27. Menotti savage or Flotow rose
28. Props for Met *Otello*, Act 3
29. Take nothing from Pasquale and he loves in Latin
30. Aspire, Miss Stevens
35. Turn Loewe gavotte into high-jumping heroine
36. Knock the H out of Chabrier king
37. 7 across set cap for him

39. Entangle this bolero composer
40. Her bolero composer was Verdi
41. Statuette for Verdi page
43. Initials for either famous Lehmann
44. Mephisto (often): '____ bien'
47. Half of a Prokofiev epic
48. Des Grieux: 'À mon ____ trop chère'
49. Iago: '____ la notte'
50. Colour of Bluebeard's first chamber

Answers

ACT I: QUIZZES

How Do You Solve a Problem Like ...?

Mimi
Aida
Rosina
Iphigénie
Amelia

Carmen
Amina
Lucia
Leonora (in either *Il Trovatore* or *La Forza del Destino*)
Anna Bolena
Santuzza

Broadway Moments

1. 'Questa o quella,' from Verdi's *Rigoletto* (alternatively, several moments in Mozart's *Don Giovanni*); Victor Herbert (lyric by Henry Blossom), *The Red Mill* (1906)

2. 'The Ride of the Valkyries,' from Wagner's *Die Walküre*; Frank Loesser, *Guys and Dolls* (1950)

3. 'Seguidilla,' from Bizet's *Carmen*; Richard Adler and Jerry Ross, *The Pajama Game* (1954)

4. 'The Jewel Song,' from Gounod's *Faust*; Leonard Bernstein (lyric by Stephen Sondheim), *West Side Story* (1957)

5. 'In questa reggia,' from Puccini's *Turandot*; Cole Porter, *Kiss Me Kate* (1948)

6. 'Quando le sere al placido,' from Verdi's *Luisa Miller*; Arthur Schwartz (lyric by Howard Dietz), *The Band Wagon* (1931)

7. 'Un bel di,' from Puccini's *Madama Butterfly*; George Gershwin (lyric by Ira Gershwin), cut from *Lady, Be Good* (1924)

8. 'The Liebesnacht,' from Wagner's *Tristan und Isolde*; Cole Porter, *Gay Divorce* (1932)

9. 'Un baccio ... un baccio ancora,' from Verdi's *Otello*; Stephen Sondheim, *Follies* (1971)

10. 'Elsa's Dream,' from Wagner's *Lohengrin*; Richard Rodgers (lyric by Oscar Hammerstein II), *Oklahoma!* (1943)

11. 'Vesti la giubba,' from Leoncavallo's *Pagliacci*; Stephen Sondheim, *A Little Night Music* (1973)

12. 'Che gelida manina,' from Puccini's *La Bohème*; Jerome Kern (lyric by Otto Harbach), *Roberta* (1933)

13. 'Voi che sapete,' from Mozart's *Le Nozze di Figaro*; Cole Porter, *Wake Up and Dream* (1929)

14. 'Die Frist ist um,' from Wagner's *The Flying Dutchman*; Jerome Kern (lyric by Oscar Hammerstein II), *Show Boat* (1927)

15. 'Mon coeur s'ouvre à toi voix,' from Saint-Saëns's *Samson et Dalila*; Richard Rodgers (lyric by Lorenz Hart), *Spring Is Here* (1929)

NOTE: There may of course be other suitable answers. And it may be worth mentioning that 'I Feel Pretty' has been warbled by Kiri Te Kanawa, 'Night and Day' by Cesare Siepi, 'One More Kiss' by Licia Albanese, 'Out of My Dreams' and 'The Touch of Your Hand' by Eleanor Steber, 'Send In the Clowns' by Renata Scotto, and 'Where's the Mate for Me?' by Jerry Hadley.

Quotable Quotes

1. Figaro in *Il Barbiere di Siviglia*
2. Leporello in *Don Giovanni*
3. Monostatos in *Die Zauberflöte*
4. Despina in *Così Fan Tutte*
5. Musetta in *La Bohème*
6. Rigoletto in *Rigoletto*
7. Leonora in *Il Trovatore*
8. Alfio in *Cavalleria Rusticana*
9. Cavaradossi in *Tosca*
10. Gutrune in *Götterdämmerung*
11. Elektra in *Elektra*
12. Wowkle in *La Fanciulla del West*
13. Wellgunde in *Das Rheingold*
14. Gurnemanz in *Parsifal*
15. Herod in *Salome*
16. Lescaut in *Manon Lescaut*
17. Manon in *Manon*
18. Tannhäuser in *Tannhäuser*
19. Arkel in *Pelléas et Mélisande*
20. Constance in *Dialogues des Carmélites*

Please, Mr Postman

1. Germont to Violetta, in *La Traviata*
2. Tatiana to Onegin, in *Eugene Onegin*
3. Dr Falke to Adele, in *Die Fledermaus*
4. La Périchole to Piquillo, in *La Périchole*
5. Macbeth to Lady Macbeth, in *Macbeth*
6. Louise to Julien, in *Louise*
7. His mother to José, recommending Micaëla, in *Carmen*
8. Carlo to Elisabetta, recommending Rodrigo, in *Don Carlo*

9. Pinkerton to Sharpless, read to Cio-Cio-San, in *Madama Butterfly*
10. Barnaba to Alvise, dictated to Isepo the Notary, in *La Gioconda*
11. Golaud to Pelléas, read by Geneviève, in *Pelléas et Mélisande*
12. Falstaff to Meg and, identically, to Alice, in *Falstaff*
13. Rosina to Almaviva, read by Figaro, in *Il Barbiere di Siviglia*
14. The Countess to the Count, dictated to Susanna, in *Le Nozze di Figaro*
15. Des Grieux to his father, read over his shoulder by Manon, in *Manon*
16. The Princess Bouillion via Duclos to Maurizio, in *Adriana Lecouvreur* (This letter is also intercepted by the Abbé and read to the Prince!)

Opera in Paris

A. *Adriana Lecouvreur*
B. *Boulevard Solitude*
C. *Cardillac*
D. *Danton and Robespierre*
E. *Esmeralda*
F. *Fedora*
G. *(The) Ghosts of Versailles*
H. *(Les) Huguenots*
I. *(The) Italian Straw Hat*
J. *Jonny Spielt Auf*
K. *Kaiserin Josephine*
L. *Lodoletta*
M. *Madeleine*
N. *Notre Dame*
O. *(Der) Opernball*
P. *Peter Ibbetson*
Q. *Quasimodo*
R. *(La) Rondine*
S. *Sapho*
T. *(The) Tsar Has His Photograph Taken*
U. *Ugo, Conte di Parigi*
V. *Véronique*
W. *(Der) Wasserträger, (The) Water Carrier*
Z. *Zazà*

NOTE: Nino Rota's original title is *Il Capello de Paglia di Firenze*. (The opera antedates his famous film scores for Fellini.) Weill's now-popular trifle was written as *Der Zar Lässt Sich Fotografieren*. Cherubini's opera, once popular under its German and English titles, was first called *Les Deux Journées*. Donizetti's *Ugo* is set mainly in Laon, before Hugh Capet moved the capital to Paris. Apologies to those who would have preferred, under the respective initial letters, *Julien*, *Linda di Chamounix*, *Madame Sans-Gêne*, *La Postillon de Longjumeau*, *Thérèse*, and *La Vie Parisienne*. Paris is certainly the favourite locale for opera plots! But it might in closing be said that many of the best operas are set in Seville.

Pairs

1. Smugglers in *Carmen*
2. Lackeys of Sir John in *Falstaff*
3. Conspirators in *Un Ballo in Maschera*
4. Plebeians in *Simon Boccanegra*
5. Runaway monks in *Boris Godunov*
6. Intriguers in *Der Rosenkavalier*
7. Stepbrothers in *Jenůfa*

8. Stepsisters in *La Cenerentola*
9. Stepsisters in *Cendrillon*
10. Guglielmo and Ferrando in disguise in *Così Fan Tutte*
11. Don Alvaro and Don Carlo under assumed names in *La Forza del Destino*
12. Count di Luna and Manrico, infant brothers in *Il Trovatore*
13. Parents in *Gianni Schicchi*
14. Married couple in *Il Tabarro*
15. Indian mates in *La Fanciulla del West*
16. East Indian slaves in *L'Africaine*
17. Married couple in *Porgy and Bess*
18. Interlocutors in *Four Saints in Three Acts*
19. Ghosts in *The Turn of the Screw*
20. Brothers in *The Gondoliers*
21. Parents in *Arabella*
22. Parents in *Daphne*
23. Rival poet and composer in *Capriccio*
24. Drinking cronies in *Werther*
25. English girls in *Lakmé*
26. Lovers in *A Village Romeo and Juliet*
27. Lovers in *The Midsummer Marriage*
28. Gay lovers in *The Knot Garden*
29. Separated lovers in *The Telephone*
30. Actors in *Adriana Lecouvreur*
31. Students in *Les Contes d'Hoffmann*
32. Student composers in *Palestrina*
33. Drunks in *Prince Igor*
34. Peasant girls in *Don Giovanni*
35. Slain warriors in *Die Walküre*

Sobriquets

1. Leonore in *Fidelio*
2. The Duke of Mantua in *Rigoletto*
3. The Count Almaviva in *Il Barbiere di Siviglia*
4. Tristan in *Tristan und Isolde*
5. Siegmund in *Die Walküre*
6. Octavian in *Der Rosenkavalier*
7. The Marschallin in *Der Rosenkavalier*
8. Madeleine de Coigny in *Andrea Chénier*
9. Garcia di Luna in *Il Trovatore*
10. Raffaele in *Le Nozze di Figaro*
11. Don Alvaro in *La Forza del Destino*
12. Don Carlo di Vargas in *La Forza del Destino*
13. Eisenstein in *Die Fledermaus*
14. Adele in *Die Fledermaus*
15. Frank in *Die Fledermaus*
16. Fiesco in *Simon Boccanegra*
17. Don Juan of Aragon in *Ernani*
18. Angelina in *Cenerentola*
19. Lucette in *Cendrillon*
20. Norina in *Don Pasquale*
21. Aminta in *Die Schweigsame Frau*
22. Sperata in *Mignon*
23. Lulu in *Lulu*
24. Alcindoro in *La Bohème*
25. John Claggart in *Billy Budd*

Love Is ...

1. Carmen in *Carmen*
2. Thaïs in *Thaïs*
3. The Duke of Mantua in *Rigoletto*
4. Alfredo in *La Traviata*
5. Aida in *Aida*
6. Falstaff and Ford in *Falstaff*
7. Andrea Chénier in *Andrea Chénier*
8. Cherubino in *Le Nozze di Figaro*
9. Zerlina in *Don Giovanni*
10. Dorabella in *Così Fan Tutte*
11. Tamino in *Die Zauberflöte*
12. Wolfram in *Tannhäuser*
13. Isolde in *Tristan und Isolde*
14. Siegmund in *Die Walküre*
15. Salome in *Salome*
16. Jupiter in *Semele*
17. Patience in *Patience*
18. The Queen of the Fairies in *Iolanthe*
19. Anne Trulove in *The Rake's Progress*
20. Aschenbach in *Death in Venice*

What Opera Are You Watching?

1. *Madame Chrysanthème*, by Messager
2. *La Bohème*, by Leoncavallo
3. *La Rondine*, by Puccini
4. *Otello*, by Rossini (his alternate ending)
5. *Die Lustigen Weiber von Windsor*, by Nicolai
6. *I Capuleti e i Montecchi*, by Bellini
7. *Leonora*, by Paer
8. *Orphée aux Enfers*, by Offenbach
9. *Ariane et Barbe-Bleue*, by Dukas
10. *Turandot*, by Busoni
11. *Hérodiade*, by Massenet
12. *Werther*, by Massenet
13. *Dimitrij*, by Dvořák
14. *Chérubin*, by Massenet
15. *La Mère Coupable*, by Milhaud
16. *The Stone Guest*, by Dargomijsky
17. *Zampa*, by Hérold
18. *Didone*, by Cavalli
19. *Mona*, by Parker
20. *Die Legende von der Heiligen Elisabeth*, by Liszt
21. *Loreley*, by Catalani
22. *Hans Heiling*, by Marschner
23. *Sigurd*, by Reyer
24. *Doktor Faust*, by Busoni
25. *Hans Sachs*, by Lortzing

NOTE: Given the operatic potential of the plays of Shakespeare and of the myths that surround Orpheus, Siegfried, Faust, and Don Juan, there may be other acceptable answers for some of the questions. But none of the operas cited here can be thought a complete rarity. All have been staged and/or recorded in recent years save perhaps *Madame Chrysanthème* (which anticipated Puccini's *Madama Butterfly* by eleven years) and *Mona* (which won a Met competition for best new American opera and received four performances there in 1912). *Sigurd* has hardly been a rarity in Paris, where it has enjoyed one hundred more performances at the Opéra than has *Götterdämmerung*. Liszt's *St Elisabeth* is an oratorio, but has been performed as an opera both at Weimar and the Met.

The Eyes Have It

1. Arnalta in *L'Incoronazione di Poppea*
2. Figaro in *Le Nozze di Figaro*
3. Don Ottavio in *Don Giovanni*
4. Guglielmo in *Così Fan Tutte*
5. Agathe in *Der Freischütz*
6. Wellgunde in *Das Rheingold*
7. Fasolt in *Das Rheingold*
8. Fricka in *Die Walküre*
9. Brünnhilde in *Die Walküre*
10. Wotan in *Siegfried*
11. Isolde in *Tristan und Isolde*
12. Walther in *Die Meistersinger*
13. Ferrando in *Il Trovatore*
14. Fra Melitone in *La Forza del Destino*
15. Barnaba in *La Gioconda*
16. Rodolfo in *La Bohème*
17. Tosca in *Tosca*
18. Boris in *Boris Godunov*
19. Escamillo in *Carmen*
20. Des Grieux in *Manon*
21. Werther in *Werther*
22. Chimène in *Le Cid*
23. Golaud in *Pelléas et Mélisande*
24. Salome in *Salome*
25. Arabella in *Arabella*

The Moon Is Like the Moon

1. Norma in *Norma*
2. Siegmund in *Die Walküre*
3. Rodolfo in *La Bohème*
4. Leonora in *Il Trovatore*
5. Monostatos in *Die Zauberflöte*
6. Yum-Yum in *The Mikado*
7. Captain Corcoran in *H.M.S. Pinafore*
8. Enzo in *La Gioconda*
9. Lucia in *Lucia di Lammermoor*
10. Cio-Cio-San in *Madama Butterfly*
11. The people of Peking in *Turandot*
12. Marie in *Wozzeck*
13. The Simpleton in *Boris Godunov*
14. Pelléas in *Pelléas et Mélisande*
15. Énée in *Les Troyens*
16. Juliette in *Roméo et Juliette*
17. Moonshine (Starveling) in *A Midsummer Night's Dream*
18. The Emperor in *Die Frau ohne Schatten*
19. Rusalka in *Rusalka*
20. Elena in *Mefistofele*
21. The Mayor in *Der Mond*
22. Jack the Ripper in *Lulu*
23. Ecclitico in *Il Mondo della Luna*
24. Brouček in *The Excursions of Mr Brouček*
25. The Page of Herodias in *Salome*

Lim'ricked Librettos

1. 'I was pure as the snow till I drifted.' (*La Traviata*, and perhaps a few others)
2. And in Act 3 there's 'Here comes the bride.' (*Lohengrin*)
3. And what's he do? Break down and crai! (*Manon Lescaut*)
4. It's Gounod's. And it ends with 'Anges purs.' (*Faust*)

5. If a lady disguised in man's pantua.
   (*Rigoletto*)
6. And she almost expires of anemia.
   (*Der Freischütz*)
7. Sans venery, sans bacchanality?'
   (*Tannhäuser*)

8. One oughtn't to read in Romance
   a lot. (*Francesca da Rimini*)
9. And sings 'Del mio dolce ardor.'
   (*Paride ed Elena*)
10. The CIA. (*Der Fliegende
    Holländer*)

Deconstruction in Dixie

In Puccini's *Gianni Schicchi*, the third part of his *Trittico*, the relatives of the newly deceased Buoso Donati enlist the services of the crafty Gianni Schicci to help them change the will. One of the relatives, Rinuccio, is in love with Gianni's daughter Lauretta. Hence:

Opera: *Johnny Squeaky*
Florida Millionaire: B.D. 'the Bozo'
Junior Mafioso: R.N. 'Okee' Pinocchio
Godfather: Johnny Squeaky
Pretty Daughter: Lauderdaletta

In Massenet's *Thaïs*, the fatherly cenobite Palemon hears that one of his charges, Athanael, has fallen in love with the Alexandrian courtesan Thaïs. Athanael finds her at the house of his former friend Nicias. Hence:

Opera: *Miss Thailand*
Old Cult Founder: Pa Lemon
Young Composer: A.T. Honeywell
Exotic Dancer: 'Thighs' of the Thailand Dance Hall
School Chum: Nicky S.

In Wagner's *Die Meistersinger von Nürnberg*, Walther von Stolzing, who learned his music from listening to songbirds, is disqualified from a singing contest by Sixtus Beckmesser, loved by Eva (the daughter of the wealthy goldsmith Veit Pogner), aided by the apprentice David and his more mature sweetheart Magdalene, and given lessons in composition by Hans Sachs, the shoemaker (Schuster). Hence:

Opera: *The Masterflingers of Baltimore*
Southpaw Kid: Walter 'From the Shoestring' Birtwistle
Team Manager: Bic 'Six Toes' Messer

Owner: 'Whitey' Goldsmith
Nubile Daughter: Evie Goldsmith
Bat Boy: David Prentiss
Female Reporter: Madge Delaney
Pitching Coach: Honus 'Sox' Schuster

NOTE: The originator of this reconstruction, John St James, chose Baltimore rather than, say, Pittsburg because of the Orioles' masterful 1971 pitching staff (Palmer, McNally, Cuellar, and Dobson), and because 'Honus' Wagner's text gamely uses the music of songbirds as a running metaphor. He notes, however, that *The Masterflingers* wouldn't be the first baseball opus on the musical stage. That honour belongs to *Faust in Pinstripes* ossia *Damn Yankees*.

Hits, Runs, and Errors

A. Henry Aaron
B. George Bell
C. Roy Campanella
D. Joe DiMaggio
E. Billy Evans
F. Nellie Fox
G. Hank Greenberg
H. Catfish Hunter
I. Monte Irvin
J. Walter Johnson
K. Mark Koenig
L. Ernie Lombardi
M. Christy Mathewson

N. Hal Newhouser
O. Mickey Owen
P. Satchel Paige
Q. Carlos Quintana
R. Babe Ruth
S. Tris Speaker
T. Joe Torre
U. Jack Urban
V. Frank Viola
W. Honus Wagner
Y. Cy Young
Z. Heinie Zimmerman

FOR THE RECORD: 'Honus' (Hans) Wagner was also known as 'The Flying Dutchman'; 'Tris' Speaker's name was Tristram; the quotations in the biographical clues are from the Hall of Fame plaques.

I Heard It at the Movies I

1. 'Nobles seigneurs, salut' and 'Une dame noble et sage,' from *Les Huguenots*. *Maytime* (1937): Nelson Eddy, Jeanette MacDonald, John Barrymore

2. 'Anges purs,' from *Faust*. *Grand Illusion* (1937): Marcel Dalio, Pierre Fresnay, Jean Gabin

3. 'Meditation,' from *Thaïs*. *Golden Boy* (1939): William Holden, Lee J. Cobb

4. Prelude to Act 1 of *Lohengrin*. *The Great Dictator* (1940): Charles Chaplin

5. 'Una voce poco fa,' from *Il Barbiere di Siviglia*. *Citizen Kane* (1941): Fortunio Bononova, Orson Welles, Dorothy Comingore

6. 'Habanera,' from *Carmen*. *Going My Way* (1944): Bing Crosby, Risë Stevens

7. 'Brindisi,' from *La Traviata*. *The Lost Weekend* (1945): Ray Milland, Jane Wyman

8. 'Liebestrank,' 'Liebesnacht,' 'Delirium,' and 'Liebestod' from *Tristan und Isolde*. *Humoresque* (1946): John Garfield (with Isaac Stern fiddling), Oscar Levant, Joan Crawford

9. 'Il mio tesoro,' from *Don Giovanni*. *Kind Hearts and Coronets* (1949): Dennis Price (as *both* Louis and his father), Alec Guinness (as *all eight* D'Ascoynes)

10. 'La donna è mobile,' from *Rigoletto*. *The Importance of Being Earnest* (1952): Michael Redgrave

11. 'Di quella pira,' from *Il Trovatore*. *Senso* (1953): Alida Valli, Farley Granger

12. 'Mon coeur s'ouvre à ta voix,' from *Samson et Dalila*. *Interrupted Melody* (1955): Eleanor Parker (with Eileen Farrell singing), Glenn Ford

13. Overture to *Le Nozze di Figaro*. *The Ipcress File* (1965)

14. 'O ew'ge Nacht,' from *Die Zauberflöte*. *Hour of the Wolf* (1967): Max von Sydow, Liv Ullmann

15. 'Dance of the Blessed Spirits,' from *Orfeo ed Euridice*. *Hot Millions* (1968): Peter Ustinov, Maggie Smith

16. 'Soave sia il vento,' from *Così Fan Tutte*. *Sunday Bloody Sunday* (1971): Peter Finch, Murray Head, Glenda Jackson (recording by Pilar Lorengar, Yvonne Minton, and Barry McDaniel)

17. 'E lucevan le stelle,' from *Tosca*. *Serpico* (1973): Al Pacino

18. 'M'apparì,' from *Martha*. *Breaking Away* (1979): Dennis Christopher

19. 'The Ride of the Valkyries,' from *Die Walküre*. *Apocalypse Now* (1979): Robert Duvall (Solti recording)

20. Intermezzo from *Guglielmo Ratcliff*. *Raging Bull* (1980): Robert De Niro

21. 'Au fond du temple saint,' from *Les Pêcheurs de Perles*. *Gallipoli* (1981): Mel Gibson (recording by Léopold Simoneau and René Bianco)

22. 'Ebben? Ne andrò lontana,' from *La Wally*. *Diva* (1982): Wilhelmenia Wiggins Fernandez

23. 'O du mein holder Abendstern,' from *Tannhäuser*. *The Night of the Shooting Stars* (1983)

24. 'Nessun dorma,' from *Turandot*. *The Killing Fields* (1984): Sam Waterston, Haing S. Ngor (recording by Franco Corelli)

25. 'Una furtiva lagrima,' from *L'Elisir d'Amore*. *Prizzi's Honor* (1985): Anjelica Huston, William Hickey

I Heard It at the Movies II

1. 'Stride la vampa' from *Il Trovatore*. *A Night at the Opera* (1935): Chico, Harpo, and Groucho Marx

2. 'Peasant Dance' from *Eugene Onegin*. *Anna Karenina* (1935): Greta Garbo and Fredric March

3. 'Caro nome' from *Rigoletto*. *I Dream Too Much* (1935): Lily Pons and Henry Fonda

4. 'Ah! la mia cara' from *Carnival*, a fragmentary opera by Oscar Levant written to a text by William Kernel for *Charlie Chan at the Opera* (1936): Warner Oland and Boris Karloff

5. 'Anges purs' from *Faust*. *San Francisco* (1936): Jeanette MacDonald, Spencer Tracy, and Clark Gable

6. Prelude to Act 1 of *Lohengrin*. *100 Men and a Girl* (1937): Deanna Durbin and Leopold Stokowski

7. 'Verrano a te sull'aure' from *Lucia di Lammermoor*. *The Flame of New Orleans* (1941): Marlene Dietrich (duet sung by Gitta Alpar and Anthony Marlowe)

8. Drinking Song from *Martha*. *The Phantom of the Opera* (1943): Claude Rains, Nelson Eddy, and Susanna Foster

9. 'Je suis Titania' from *Mignon*. *The Life and Death of Colonel Blimp* (1943): Roger Livesey, Deborah Kerr, and Anton Walbrook

10. 'Là ci darem la mano' from *Don Giovanni*. *The Picture of Dorian Gray* (1945): George Sanders, Hurd Hatfield, and Angela Lansbury

11. 'O terra, addio' from *Aida*. *The Great Caruso* (1951): Richard Hageman, Mario Lanza, Dorothy Kirsten, and Ann Blyth (Caruso actually made his Met debut in *Rigoletto*, conducted by Arturo Vigna, with Marcella Sembrich.)

12. Final scene from *Salome*. *The Man Between* (1953): Ljuba Welitsch, James Mason, and Claire Bloom.

13. Overture to *Il Barbiere di Siviglia*. *8½* (1963): Marcello Mastroianni

14. Act 1 duet ('Was mich berückt') from *Die Walküre*. *That Obscure Object of Desire* (1977) (Karl Böhm recording with Leonie Rysanek and James King) (The 'Conchita' story, long considered as a subject by Puccini, was finally treated by Zandonai.)

15. 'Casta diva' from *Norma*. *Atlantic City* (1981): Burt Lancaster and Susan Sarandon (aria sung by Elisabeth Harwood)

16. Final scene from *Ernani*. *Fitzcarraldo* (1982): Klaus Kinski and Claudia Cardinale (scene sung by Mietta Sighele, Veriano Luchetti, and Dimiter Petkov)

17. 'L'ho perduta' from *Le Nozze di Figaro*. *Kaos* (1985)

18. 'Chi il bel sogno di Doretta' from *La Rondine*. *Room with a View* (1986) (aria sung by Kiri Te Kanawa)

19. Final scene from *Madama Butterfly*. *Fatal Attraction* (1987): Glenn Close and Michael Douglas (scene sung by Mirella Freni and Luciano Pavarotti, Herbert von Karajan conducting)

20. 'Dance of the Apprentices' from *Die Meistersinger*. *Hope and Glory* (1987)

21. Act 3 scene ('Bada, sotto il guanciale') from *La Bohème*. *Moonstruck* (1987): Nicolas Cage, Cher, Olympia Dukakis, Vincent Gardenia, and Feodor Chaliapin, Jr (scene sung by Renata Tebaldi and Carlo Bergonzi, acted by Martha Collins and John Fanning)

22. 'Son vergin vezzosa' from *I Puritani*. *The Dead* (1987)

23. 'Song to the Moon' from *Rusalka*. *Driving Miss Daisy* (1989): Jessica Tandy, Morgan Freeman, and Dan Aykroyd (aria sung by Gabriela Beňačková)

24. 'Amami, Alfredo'; opening and closing music from *La Traviata*. *Pretty Woman* (1990): Richard Gere and Julia Roberts (sung by Karin Calabro, arranged by Thomas Pasatieri)

25. Easter chorus from *Cavalleria Rusticana*. *The Godfather III* (1990): Al Pacino and Diane Keaton (music supervised by Anton Coppola)

I Heard It at the Movies III

1. 'Anges purs' from *Faust*. *Metropolitan* (1935): Lawrence Tibbett and Virginia Bruce

2. Sextet from *Lucia di Lammermoor*. *Captain January* (1936): Guy Kibbee, Shirley Temple, and Slim Summerville

3. Final scene from *Tosca*. *Rose Marie* (1936): Jeanette MacDonald and Nelson Eddy

4. Finale (expanded to an MGM potpourri) from *Die Fledermaus*. *The Great Waltz* (1938): Luise Rainer, Fernand Gravet, and Miliza Korjus

5. 'The Dance of the Hours' from *La Gioconda*. *Fantasia* (1940): Deems Taylor and Leopold Stokowski

6. Closing scene from *Salammbô*, a fragmentary opera by Bernard Hermann written to order for *Citizen Kane* (1941): Dorothy Comingore, Orson Welles, and Joseph Cotten

7. 'Di Provenza' from *La Traviata*. *Ossessione* (based on *The Postman Always Rings Twice*) (1942)

8. Pilgrims' Chorus from *Tannhäuser*. *Hi Diddle Diddle* (1943): Pola Negri

9. Liebestod from *Tristan und Isolde*. *Christmas Holiday* (1944): Deanna Durbin and Gene Kelly

10. Prize Song from *Die Meistersinger*. *Two Sisters from Boston* (1946): Lauritz Melchior, June Allyson, and Kathryn Grayson

11. 'Dance of the Blessed Spirits' from *Orphée et Eurydice*. *Orphée* (1949): Jean Marais and Maria Casarès

12. Coronation Scene from *Boris Godunov*. *Tonight We Sing* (1953): Ezio Pinza (singing in Russian) and David Wayne. The Final Scene, the death of Boris, is a valid alternative answer

13. 'Three little maids from school' from *The Mikado*. *Chariots of Fire* (1981): Ben Cross and Alice Krige.

14. 'Nessun dorma' from *Turandot*. *Yes, Giorgio* (1982): Luciano Pavarotti

15. 'O patria mia' from *Aida*. *And the Ship Sails On* (1984)

16. 'Ein Mädchen oder Weibchen' [A sweetheart or a pretty little wife] from *Die Zauberflöte*. *Amadeus* (1984): Tom Hulce, Simon Callow (who played Hulce's role in stage original), F. Murray Abraham (aria sung by Brian Kay, Neville Marriner conducting)

17. Good Friday Spell from *Parsifal*. *Kiss of the Spider Woman* (1985): William Hurt, Raul Julia, and Sonia Braga

18. 'Va, pensiero' from *Nabucco*. *The Color of Money* (1986): Paul Newman and Tom Cruise

19. Opening measures of *Madama Butterfly*. *Hannah and Her Sisters* (1986): Sam Waterston, Dianne Wiest, and Carrie Fisher

20. 'Vesti la giubba' from *Pagliacci*. *The Untouchables* (1987): Robert De Niro and Sean Connery (recording: Mario Del Monaco)

21. 'Largo al factotum' from *Il Barbiere di Siviglia*. *Mrs. Doubtfire* (1993): Robin Williams

22. 'La mamma morta' from *Andrea Chénier*. *Philadelphia* (1993): Denzel Washington and Tom Hanks (recording: Maria Callas)

23. Letter Duet from *Le Nozze di Figaro*. *The Shawshank Redemption* (1994): Tim Robbins and Morgan Freeman (recording: Edith Mathis and Gundula Janowitz, Karl Böhm conducting)

24. 'Deh vieni alla finestra' from *Don Giovanni*. *La Cérémonie* (1996): Sandrine Bonnaire, Isabelle Huppert, and Jacqueline Bisset.

25. The Flight of the Bumble Bee from *Tsar Saltan*. *Shine* (1996): Geoffrey Rush

ACT II: ANAGRAMS

Donna Anagram

Alberich	Norma
Bardolph	Olympia
Coppélius	Parsifal
Dodon	Quasimodo
Enzo Grimaldo	Remendado
Fasolt	Spoletta
Gunther	Tannhäuser
Herodias	Ulrica
Isolde	Venus
Juliette	Woglinde
Kaspar	Xerxes
Laertes	Yniold
Melitone	Zerlina

Fan Anagrams

A. Luigi ALVA
B. Agnes BALTSA
C. Maria CALLAS
D. Plácido DOMINGO
E. Florence EASTON
F. Kirsten FLAGSTAD
G. Tito GOBBI
H. Jerome HINES
I. Maria IVOGÜN
J. Marcel JOURNET
K. Roberta KNIE
L. Evelyn LEAR
M. Nellie MELBA

N. Lillian NORDICA
O. Magda OLIVERO
P. Aureliano PERTILE
Q. Louis QUILICO
R. Rosa RAISA
S. Risë STEVENS
T. Renata TEBALDI
U. Viorica URSULEAC
V. Astrid VARNAY
W. Wolfgang WINDGASSEN
Y. Janice YOES
Z. Giovanni ZENATELLO

Academic Patter

Peter Cornelius, *The Barber of Bagdad*

Titurel

Hedwig

Edgar

Barbieri

Abul Hassan

Rattle

Blitzstein

Elvino

Ramey

Oscar

Fricka

Barrientos

Amonasro

Gastone

Dappertutto

Amfortas

Désormière

NOTE: The high point of Cornelius's opera is Abul Hassan's patter song, 'Bin Akademiker.'

ACT III: VERTICAL PATTERNS

Vertical Patterns 1

1	M	O	R	I	R	S	I	P	U	R	A	E	B	E	L	L	A
2	M	O	R	I	R	T	R	E	M	E	N	D	A	C	O	S	A
3	M	I	R	I	S	T	S	O	W	U	N	D	E	R	B	A	R
4	M	A	R	T	E	R	N	A	L	L	E	R	A	R	T	E	N
5	D	E	H	V	I	E	N	I	N	O	N	T	A	R	D	A	R
6	A	H	F	U	G	G	I	I	L	T	R	A	D	I	T	O	R
7	A	H	F	U	Y	E	Z	D	O	U	C	E	I	M	A	G	E
8	I	L	L	A	C	E	R	A	T	O	S	P	I	R	I	T	O
9	I	L	E	S	T	D	O	U	X	I	L	E	S	T	B	O	N
10	S	O	L	E	N	N	E	I	N	Q	U	E	S	T	O	R	A
11	P	I	G	E	O	N	S	O	N	T	H	E	G	R	A	S	S
12	O	D	E	L	M	I	O	D	O	L	C	E	A	R	D	O	R
13	N	E	M	I	C	O	D	E	L	L	A	P	A	T	R	I	A
14	D	E	H	P	R	O	T	E	G	G	I	M	I	O	D	I	O
15	T	E	S	C	H	E	K	B	E	D	I	E	N	D	I	C	H
16	W	E	I	C	H	E	W	O	T	A	N	W	E	I	C	H	E
17	Q	U	I	L	A	V	O	C	E	S	U	A	S	O	A	V	E
18	D	A	M	O	R	S	U	L	L	A	L	I	R	O	S	E	E
19	W	A	R	E	S	S	O	S	C	H	M	A	H	L	I	C	H
20	O	Q	U	A	L	S	O	A	V	E	B	R	I	V	I	D	O
21	U	N	A	F	U	R	T	I	V	A	L	A	G	R	I	M	A
22	O	M	A	L	Y	R	E	I	M	M	O	R	T	E	L	L	E
23	O	L	E	G	E	R	E	H	I	R	O	N	D	E	L	L	E
24	I	G	O	T	P	L	E	N	T	Y	O	N	U	T	T	I	N
25	E	S	C	H	E	R	Z	O	D	E	F	O	L	L	I	A	
26	N	O	U	S	V	I	V	R	O	N	S	A	P	A	R	I	S

The artist specially remembered is LEONARD WARREN, who died onstage during the Metropolitan Opera performance of *La Forza del Destino* on 4 March 1960 after singing the recitative and aria 'Morir! tremenda cosa!' (To die! A tremendous thing!)

Vertical Patterns II

1	L	A	S	C	I	A	C	H	I	O	P	I	A	N	G	A
2	L	A	S	C	I	A	T	E	M	I	M	O	R	I	R	E
3	U	N	A	V	O	L	T	A	C	E	R	A	U	N	R	E
4	S	T	R	A	N	G	E	A	D	V	E	N	T	U	R	E
5	S	T	E	L	L	A	D	E	L	M	A	R	I	N	A	R
6	S	E	L	I	G	W	I	E	D	I	E	S	O	N	N	E
7	D	E	H	C	O	N	T	E	L	I	P	R	E	N	D	I
8	A	M	F	O	R	T	A	S	D	I	E	W	U	N	D	E
9	E	N	F	E	R	M	A	N	T	L	E	S	Y	E	U	X
10	E	N	V	A	I	N	P	O	U	R	E	V	I	T	E	R
11	S	I	T	U	M	A	I	M	E	S	C	A	R	M	E	N
12	W	I	T	H	C	A	T	L	I	K	E	T	R	E	A	D
13	H	E	I	S	A	N	E	N	G	L	I	S	H	M	A	N
14	S	C	I	N	T	I	L	L	E	D	I	A	M	A	N	T
15	Z	W	E	I	T	E	B	R	A	U	T	N	A	C	H	T
16	Q	U	E	S	T	A	E	L	A	Q	U	E	R	C	I	A
17	R	E	C	O	N	D	I	T	A	A	R	M	O	N	I	A
18	C	H	E	V	I	T	A	M	A	L	E	D	E	T	T	A
19	G	L	O	I	R	E	I	M	M	O	R	T	E	L	L	E
20	E	L	U	C	E	V	A	N	L	E	S	T	E	L	L	E
21	P	A	R	L	E	M	O	I	D	E	M	A	M	E	R	E
22	S	O	N	V	E	R	G	I	N	V	E	Z	Z	O	S	A
23	S	O	G	N	O	S	O	A	V	E	E	C	A	S	T	O
24	T	U	L	A	M	I	A	S	T	E	L	L	A	S	E	I
25	T	U	T	U	P	I	C	C	O	L	O	I	D	D	I	O

The artist saluted is LUCINE AMARA, who is so well remembered for her singing of the phrases on lines 6 and 25, and for her response to the request on line 21.

Vertical Patterns III

1	D	I	P	R	O	V	E	N	Z	A	I	L	M	A	R
2	D	O	N	N	A	N	O	N	V	I	D	I	M	A	I
3	C	O	N	N	A	I	S	T	U	L	E	P	A	Y	S
4	A	M	O	I	L	E	S	P	L	A	I	S	I	R	S
5	A	D	D	I	O	D	E	L	P	A	S	S	A	T	O
6	E	L	L	A	G	I	A	M	M	A	I	M	A	M	O
7	L	A	C	I	D	A	R	E	M	L	A	M	A	N	O
8	L	A	R	G	O	A	L	F	A	C	T	O	T	U	M
9	C	H	E	G	E	L	I	D	A	M	A	N	I	N	A
10	E	I	L	S	O	L	D	E	L	L	A	N	I	M	A
11	D	I	T	E	A	L	L	A	G	I	O	V	I	N	E
12	R	I	T	O	R	N	A	V	I	N	C	I	T	O	R
13	O	M	I	O	B	A	B	B	I	N	O	C	A	R	O
14	O	N	L	Y	M	A	K	E	B	E	L	I	E	V	E
15	F	I	N	C	H	H	A	N	D	E	L	V	I	N	O
16	M	E	S	L	O	N	G	S	C	H	E	V	E	U	X
17	S	E	I	L	P	A	D	R	E	P	E	R	D	E	I
18	T	R	I	N	K	E	L	I	E	B	S	C	H	E	N
19	G	L	I	T	T	E	R	A	N	D	B	E	G	A	Y
20	N	O	W	T	H	E	G	R	E	A	T	B	E	A	R
21	N	O	N	S	O	P	I	U	C	O	S	A	S	O	N
22	N	O	N	S	I	A	T	E	R	I	T	R	O	S	I
23	I	N	U	T	I	L	E	S	R	E	G	R	E	T	S
24	K	L	A	N	G	E	D	E	R	H	E	I	M	A	T
25	O	S	O	A	V	E	F	A	N	C	I	U	L	L	A

The artist to whom this quiz is dedicated is TITO GOBBI.

Vertical Patterns IV

1	H	A	B	M	I	R	S	G	E	L	O	B	T
2	H	A	I	B	E	N	R	A	G	I	O	N	E
3	D	I	E	S	E	R	A	B	S	T	A	N	D
4	I	C	H	S	A	H	D	A	S	K	I	N	D
5	E	I	N	S	A	M	W	A	C	H	E	N	D
6	D	U	B	I	S	T	D	E	R	L	E	N	Z
7	H	E	R	E	S	A	H	O	W	D	E	D	O
8	W	E	R	E	I	T	H	Y	B	R	I	D	E
9	F	A	R	E	W	E	L	L	M	Y	O	W	N
10	M	I	R	A	N	V	E	R	T	R	A	U	T
11	D	O	R	E	S	T	E	D	A	I	A	C	E
12	D	E	R	H	O	L	L	E	R	A	C	H	E
13	O	V	O	T	O	T	R	E	M	E	N	D	O
14	M	Y	M	A	N	S	G	O	N	E	N	O	W
15	M	A	L	H	E	U	R	E	U	X	R	O	I
16	G	E	L	I	E	B	T	E	R	K	O	M	M
17	V	E	S	T	I	L	A	G	I	U	B	B	A
18	U	N	A	U	R	A	A	M	O	R	O	S	A
19	I	N	A	F	F	I	A	L	U	G	O	L	A
20	U	N	A	V	O	C	E	P	O	C	O	F	A
21	S	A	N	T	O	D	I	P	A	T	R	I	A
22	S	T	R	I	D	E	L	A	V	A	M	P	A
23	E	S	O	G	N	O	O	R	E	A	L	T	A
24	P	L	A	C	I	D	O	E	I	L	M	A	R
25	N	O	N	P	I	U	D	I	F	I	O	R	I

The founding editor to whom this quiz is dedicated is IRENE SLOAN.

ACT IV: CROSTICS

Operacrostic

Andrew Porter, *Music of Three Seasons: 1974–1977* (New York: Farrar, Straus and Giroux 1978), p. 50, describing the entertainments provided by the Opéra-Comique a century ago:

'Great works of literature and fashionable novelettes alike passed under the fingers of seasoned professional librettists ... to be trimmed ... for the taste of a bourgeois public that liked to laugh a little and cry a little ... and ... go away with some graceful, pretty tunes to remember.'

A. Attila
B. Notte di luna
C. Dew Fairy
D. Rigoletto
E. Egk
F. W(illiam) W(eaver)
G. Palestrina
H. Odets
I. Rosee
J. Tibbett
K. Ecco
L. Ruffo
M. Mariette Bey
N. Ut
O. Sophie
P. Imps

Q. Cinderellas
R. Odabella
S. Fasolt, Fafner
T. Tullio Serafin
U. Hugh the Drover
V. Remus
W. Emmy Destinn
X. Eggerth, Kiepura
Y. Sadko
Z. Elsa of Brabant
a. Agathe
b. Stretto
c. Ost
d. Nello
e. Sts.

NOTE ON DEFINITION b: Stretto is 'used alternatively with stretta, to indicate a faster tempo at a point of climax, particularly in an operatic finale' (*The Norton/Grove Concise Encyclopedia of Music.* New York 1988).

Texaco Presents

Paul Jackson, *Saturday (Afternoons) at the Old Met* (Portland: Amadeus Press 1992), p. 328, referring to the first quizmaster:

'(Olin) Downes' manner was short on the urbanity associated with his son, later quizmaster Edward ... "Now this is a humdinger, so watch out ... It just bamboozles me as I look at it."'

A. Jeritza
B. Allen
C. Cross
D. Kahn
E. Sí
F. On the Air
G. Nessun dorma
H. Swarthout
I. *Aida*
J. Tibbett
K. USO
L. Robinson
M. Dawn

N. AWOL
O. Youth
P. Asti's
Q. The quiz
R. Twist
S. High D
T. Eros
U. Otis
V. Low A
W. Dom
X. McEwen
Y. Emma
Z. 'Tis

The Tenor of His Time

Michael Scott, *The Great Caruso* (New York: Alfred A. Knopf 1988), p. xi.

'The title I have chosen for my book ... was the unique sobriquet used to describe the tenor in his day ... There is, notwithstanding MGM, only one great Caruso ... I have ventured to put the shoe back on the right foot.'

A. My story
B. Is brief
C. Cheek
D. High B
E. Anton
F. Ei (egg)
G. *Les Huguenots*
H. Shoot
I. Christmas Eve
J. Ombra
K. *The Vow*
L. Twenty
M. Toi

N. Hip
O. Eh quoi
P. Gadski
Q. Rachel, quand du Seigneur
R. Et
S. Abott
T. Tenth
U. Cottone
V. Ah non
W. Roof
X. Udite
Y. Studenti
Z. Over There

NOTE ON DEFINITION D: In his recordings, Caruso transposed 'Che gelida manina' down a semitone, so as 'to take the climactic high note, now a top B, fortissimo and in full verismo style' (Scott, p. 59).

Tenors, Baritones, and Basses

Helena Matheopoulos, *Divo* (New York: Harper and Row 1986), page xiii.

'All the baritones agree that the difficulties in the title role of *Rigoletto* are not specifically vocal but also scenic, i.e., have to do with the hunchback position they are forced to adopt on stage, which makes it hard for them to make proper use of their diaphragms.'

A. He

B. Elsa, ich liebe dich

C. Lyric

D. È la solita storia

E. Non ti scordar di me

F. Allegretto

G. Méphistophélès

H. Away

I. The King of the High C's

J. Hotter

K. Effetto

L. Oder Weibchen

M. Pappataci

N. Ottokar

O. Up

P. L(enus) C(arlson),
   L(éon) C(arvalho),
   L(uigi) C(herubini)

Q. Offenbach

R. Salut, demeure

S. Doktor Faust

T. In höchster Noth

U. Vittoria, vittoria

V. Of the game

Tutti Frutti

(Gary) Schmidgall, *Literature as Opera* (New York: Oxford University Press 1977), p. 390:

'Woman's Liberation may put *Così fan tutte* on the defensive again. We should note, however, that ... *Così* is a sequel to *Le Nozze*, in which the frailty and arrogance of men in love are the focus. Mozart and Da Ponte might well have ... called their *Figaro* opera *Così fan tutti*.'

A. Shaw

B. Constanze

C. Hoffmann

D. *Mitridate*

E. Ireland

F. Die Wahrheit

G. Gueden

H. Alle

I. *Lucio*

J. *Lo Sposo Deluso*

K. Lotte

L. I want

M. *The Obligation of the First Commandment*

N. Echt

O. Roswaenge

P. Alto

Q. Tovey

R. Unite

S. Requite

T. Ezio Pinza

U. Ach, ich fühl's

V. Soyer

w. O ew'ge Nacht

x. Porretta

y. Evviva

z. Raaff

a. Anna

NOTE ON DEFINITION M: The eleven-year-old Mozart's *Die Schuldigkeit des Ersten Gebotes* (*The Obligation of the First Commandment*), subtitled *ein geistliches Singspiel* (a sacred music drama), is included in both William Mann's *The Operas of Mozart* and Charles Osborne's *The Complete Operas of Mozart*.

Napoleon Redivivus

Stendhal, *Life of Rossini*, trans. Richard N. Coe (London: Calder and Boyars 1970), p. i.

'Napoleon is dead; but a new conqueror has already shown himself to the world ... The fame of this hero knows no bounds save those of civilization itself; and he is not yet thirty-two!'

A. Seville

B. Thisbe

C. Ermione

D. Ninetta

E. Dotty

F. Haunt

G. Ah! qual colpo

H. Ladder

I. Lazy

J. Intense

K. Faddish

L. E(rmanno) W(olf)-F(errari)

M. Otto

N. Father and mother

O. Row W

P. Oh che (giorno)

Q. Shootist

R. Show business

S. Ivanoff

T. New York

U. Io sono

A Dissenting View

(Gabriele) Baldini, *The Story of Giuseppe Verdi*, trans. Roger Parker (Cambridge: Cambridge University Press 1980), p. 71 – a very novel view of Verdi's best-known librettists:

'Piave['s] ... libretti ... are much finer ... than Boito's – simply because, in detail as well as in general shape, Verdi himself composed them ... Piave was undoubtedly much more intelligent than Boito in artistic matters. Boito ... never fully understood Verdi and so continually tried to bend him towards his own ideas.'

A. Budden

B. Ah sì, ben mio

C. L'altra notte

D. Debuts

E. Isis

F. Notte densa

G. Immenso Fthà

H. Tebaldi

I. Hecate

J. Ernani, involami

K. Schiller

L. *The Merry Wives*

M. *Of Windsor*

N. Rescigno

O. Yuste

P. Out, damned spot

Q. Forty-two

R. Ghiaurov

S. I vow it

T. Urban

U. Sutherland

V. Esultate

W. Placid

X. Philippe

Y. Emmy Destinn

Z. Vecchio

a. Età

b. Rossi-Lemeni

c. Dal labbro

d. Il dì

Verdi on Wagner

M(arcello) Conati, editor and annotator, *Encounters with Verdi* (Ithaca, NY: Cornell University Press 1984), p. 329.

'When I asked him which of Wagner's works stood nearest to his heart, ... Verdi replied: "The work which always arouses my greatest admiration is *Tristan*. This gigantic structure fills me time and time again with astonishment and awe, and I still cannot quite comprehend that it was conceived and written by a human being."'

A. Maddalena

B. *Communication to My Friends*

C. O qual soave

D. New staged

E. Assassini

F. Twenty-eight

G. Isolde

H. Ebb, flow

I. Night Watchman

J. Chi del gitano

K. Operetta and Drama

L. Urlus

M. New York

N. Tristan, Tantris

O. Ettori

P. Ritt

Q. Schumann-Heink

R. Wahn, Wahn

S. Ich war, wo

T. Tichatschek

U. High Priest

V. Vittime

W. Ediths

X. Ridesta

Y. *Die Meistersinger*

Z. I was where

NOTE ON DEFINITION Y: The quotation is taken from the above source, p. 345.

His Master's Voice

Martin Gregor-Dellin, *Richard Wagner: His Life, His Work, His Century*, trans. J. Maxwell Brownjohn (San Diego, Calif.: Harcourt Brace Jovanovich 1983), p. 144.

'Despite his preoccupation with death, Wagner never rushed things. His approach to composition took its deliberate tempo from a century accustomed to thinking on a grand scale. He ... knew what the future could yet bring forth. "You dare to bark at the great Wagner?" he once demanded of Peps, his dog.'

A. Masetto
B. Aegisth
C. Rights of
D. Treptow
E. I hate men
F. Neptune
G. Gwyneth
H. Rocco
I. Edo de Waart
J. Gherardino
K. Oedipus
L. Ruhe, du Gott
M. Depends
N. Eros
O. Leukippos
P. Liebesnacht

Q. If
R. Nanki-Poo
S. Row K
T. Inaffia
U. Cotrubas
V. Happy
W. Ashby
X. Rache! Tod! Tod!
Y. Docked
Z. Wittich
a. Ah, che la morte
b. *Götterdämmerung*
c. Nothung
d. Evanescent
e. Richter

It's in the Cards

L(anfranco) Rasponi, *The Last Prima Donnas* (New York: Alfred A. Knopf 1982), p. 14.

'It is very strange that every prima donna longs to take a crack at Carmen, for it is one of the most ungrateful roles ever written. No one is ever right for the critics or the public; she is either too much a slut or too much a lady. And the audience's big applause is always reserved for the three other characters.'

A. Ludovic Halévy
B. Risë Stevens
C. Arkhipova
D. Swarthout
E. Pierrette
F. Octet
G. Notte e

H. It's you
I. The Toreador Song
J. Harry Belafonte
K. Emma Calvé
L. Librettisti
M. August
N. Sir Thomas

O. The Flower Song   U. Duct
P. Près des remparts   V. Ochre
Q. Regina Resnik   W. Neither
R. Irene Dalis   X. No thoroughfare
S. Marilyn Horne   Y. Affetto
T. Acciaccatura   Z. Schech

Depravity

Joseph Kerman, *Opera as Drama* (New York: Alfred A. Knopf 1956), p. 254, and
long a passage of considerable notoriety:
   '*Tosca*, that shabby little shocker, is no doubt admired nowadays mostly in the
gallery. In the parterre it is agreed that *Turandot* is Puccini's finest work ... it is a
good deal more depraved, and the adjective is carefully chosen.'

A. Just   N. Patatrac!
B. Orfeo   O. E lucevan le stelle
C. Stravinsky   P. Ricci brothers
D. Euridice   Q. A(lfredo) G(ermont);
E. Playwright   A(melita) G(alli-Curci)
F. Haydn   R. Addio del passato
G. Kind   S. Schonberg
H. Edited   T. Debussy
I. Rhythmed   U. Row F
J. Menotti   V. André
K. Ah, taci   W. Metastasio
L. *Nitteti*   X. Adonis
M. *Othello*

Facing the Enigmas

Ethan Mordden, *The Splendid Art of Opera* (New York: Methuen 1980), pp. 321–2.
   'Great Turandots have been few – Maria Nemeth; the superb Eva Turner ...;
Gina Cigna, the only Italian in the list; Maria Callas, who pointed her not-that-
sizable voice to capture the evil glint in the eye of the sound; and Birgit Nilsson,
Turner's only rival as all-time supreme Turandot.'

A. Eri   E. Net
B. Tu   F. Milanov
C. High F   G. Ochs
D. Austria   H. Rataplan

I. Daniel Webster
J. *Diana von Solange*
K. Egypt
L. Nicholas Vogel
M. Tutte
N. Huehn
O. Ebe
P. Schlemil
Q. Putti
R. Lotte Lehmann
S. Elemer
T. Nessler
U. Downes

V. Iris
W. Donizetti
X. Alti
Y. Rethberg
Z. *Tannhäuser*
a. Our
b. Franchetti
c. Ormandy
d. Pavarotti
e. Eye
f. Rubini
g. Attavanti

The German Composer and the American Soldier

William Mann, *Richard Strauss* (New York: Oxford University Press 1966), p. 142, on the day in 1945 'when the liberating troops walked up the drive of No. 2 Maximilianstrasse, Garmisch-Partenkirchen, [and] were met by an old man':

'Could any musician convey his identity to a foreign soldier? Strauss gambled on the popularity of one work ... "I am the composer of *Der Rosenkavalier*," he said, and the soldiers knew what [he] meant ... so much a part of inherited culture was the opera he had written.'

A. Wie du warst
B. Ich will nicht
C. Leukippos
D. Lummer
E. Io
F. Aithra
G. Myth
H. Mandryka
I. Ariadne
J. Nodded off
K. Nero
L. Resi
M. Ihre

N. Composer
O. Hugo von Hofmannsthal
P. *Aegyptische Helena*
Q. Reiner
R. *Die Frau ohne Schatten*
S. Soot
T. Taupe
U. Robert
V. Adelaide
W. United States
X. Swarowsky
Y. *Sotto voce*

Britten Waives the Rules

Alan Blyth, *Remembering Britten* (London: Hutchinson 1981), p. 22.
   'Britten's home life ran, in Sir Peter's words, along "fairly sure rails." "Ben was no Bohemian. He adhered to a regular life, beginning with a cold bath in the morning ... In domestic matters he was somewhat at a loss. He could make a cup of tea, boil an egg and wash up, but not much more. If he made his bed, he usually made a mess of it."'

A. Auden	O. Balstrode
B. Lighting a sea	P. E(rnest) A(nsermet)
C. *A Midsummer Night's Dream*	Q. Red Whiskers
D. Norman Chaffinch	R. I am finished with
E. Bob Boles	S. Nonesuch
F. Lute songs	T. *Gloriana*
G. Yes, but	U. Babe
H. *The Turn of the Screw*	V. Row AA
I. High A	W. I am an old man
J. Raw	X. *The Little Sweep*
K. Emil Cooper	Y. *The Borough*
L. Maupassant	Z. East
M. Eerie I find it	a. *Noye's Fludde*
N. Malo, Malo	

The Twentieth-Century Composer Speaks

M(ichael) Tippett, *Moving into Aquarius* (St Albans: Paladin Books 1974), p. 148.
   'I am a composer. That is someone who imagines sounds ... The outside world with all its troubles goes on around my personal sanctuary ... And I face continually a question within this paradox: has the reality of my imagination any lasting relation to the reality of those events which immediately affect the lives of men?'

A. Madame	K. Voodoo
B. Thomson	L. Italo
C. Impressionist	M. *News of the Day*
D. Passacaglia	N. Goose
E. Puff	O. Ilion
F. Emil	P. Noye
G. Twentieth century	Q. *The Cunning Little Vixen*
H. *The Italian Straw Hat*	R. Olheim
I. *Mahabharata*	S. Actium
J. *Odyssey*	T. Quint

U. Uhde
V. Amor
W. *Rise and Fall of the City of Mahagonny*

X. It Ain't Necessarily So
Y. Under the Willow Tree
Z. Sosostris

The Old and the New

G(eorge) Martin, *The Opera Companion to Twentieth-Century Opera* (New York: Dodd, Mead and Company 1979), p. 6.

'Opera could do more with symbols than spoken drama, for it was opera's peculiar quality that the orchestra could contradict a singer's expressed thoughts or indicate his subconscious fears and hopes. Opera ... was in a position to absorb easily the discoveries of the century's most startling new science, psychoanalysis.'

A. *Goyescas*
B. *Moses and Aron*
C. Addison
D. Ricciarelli
E. Tacit
F. If you want to know who
G. Nacht und Tag
H. Tilson Thomas
I. Wasps
J. *Esther*
K. Nose
L. The Mississippi
M. Io t'abbraccio
N. Edda

O. *The Crucible*
P. Hop, hop
Q. Cerha
R. Espresso
S. Nilssons
T. *Tote Stadt*
U. Ulysses
V. Richard Mohr
W. You're
X. Opera Quarterly
Y. *Porgy and Bess*
Z. *Excursions of*
a. Ralf
b. Accentuate the Positive

NOTE ON DEFINITION B: Schoenberg was so superstitious about the number 13 that, when he realized that there were thirteen letters in his title *Moses und Aaron*, he subtracted an 'a' from Aaron's name. In English that 'a' has usually been restored. But here, at least, we're honouring the composer's intentions.

ACT V: CROSSWORDS

Opera Cruise

A	T	L	A	N	T	I	C	O	C	E	A	N
V	U	■	S	■	U	S	O	■	A	■	L	O
A	R	C	S	■	T	E	X	■	D	A	W	N
■	N	O	U	S	■	P	■	L	E	D	A	■
S	E	E	R	■	T	O	M	■	T	O	Y	E
O	R	■	■	D	U	■	I	L	■	■	S	D
M	■	S	H	A	R	P	L	E	S	S	■	G
M	M	■	■	S	C	■	E	G	■	■	S	A
A	I	D	A	■	O	P	S	■	M	E	E	R
■	N	U	I	T	■	E	■	B	A	L	L	■
A	N	O	N	■	A	T	E	■	N	O	I	A
R	I	■	S	■	L	E	E	■	O	■	K	N
M	E	D	I	T	E	R	R	A	N	E	A	N

Bell-Shaped Tones

K	O	R	N	G	O	L	D		M	I	M	E
	D		U		B		E		A		S	
P	E	A	R	S		A	M	A	D	E	U	S
U		U		O		H		M		A		O
B	U	S	O	N	I		T	O	U	R	E	L
	N		P		M		O		N		N	
P	A	N	S		P	H	I	L	E	M	O	N
O		O		S			O		A		R	
P	O	S	E	I	D	O	N		E	R	D	A
	W		R		I		O		L		O	
A	L	V	I	S	E		H	A	M	L	E	T
N		I		U		E		R		A		I
D	E	L	I	L	A	H		M	I	D	A	S
	V		C		L		O		C		M	
P	E	R	I		S	C	H	L	E	M	I	L

Aria Crossword

A	D	D	I	O	D	E	L	P	A	S	S	A	T	O
R	O	I	S	■	O	L	E	A	N	■	T	R	E	U
I	O	N	■	A	M	I	■	O	N	E	■	M	A	R
A	M	O	I	L	E	S	P	L	A	I	S	I	R	S
■	■	V	■	■	E	N	O	■	■	T	■	■	■	■
■	T	R	O	P	E	■	■	A	P	R	I	L	■	■
L	A	R	G	O	A	L	F	A	C	T	O	T	U	M
■	B	A	U	E	R	■	■	T	O	Z	Z	I	■	■
■	■	E	■	■	J	O	E	■	■	Z	■	■	■	■
D	O	N	N	A	N	O	N	V	I	D	I	M	A	I
O	W	E	■	S	U	N	■	A	P	E	■	A	R	S
P	E	W	S	■	M	A	M	M	A	■	U	L	N	A
E	N	T	W	E	I	H	T	E	G	O	T	T	E	R

NOTES ON DOWN 24, 56, 58: The soprano who introduced 'Climb Ev'ry Mountain' was Patricia Neway. Mrs James McCracken was Sandra Warfield. Milanov's teacher was Milka Ternina. Ponselle's Adalgisa was Marion Telva.

La Triviata

S	I	E	B	E	L		M		F	E	D	O	R	A
T	O	M		B	E		E		R	L		S	A	N
E	S	P		B	E	R	T	R	A	M		R	N	G
V	O	I			T	R	A				I	C	E	
A	N	A	T	O	L		O		M	A	R	C	E	L
		O	R	A		P		A	M	I				
		M	E	S		O		P	A	S				
T	A	L	B	O	T		L		S	T	E	R	E	O
O	R	O		L	I	E			A	L	S			
S	T	R		W	A	L	T	H	E	R		V	E	C
C	U	I		A	M		A		R	E		E	N	A
A	S	S	U	R	E		N		A	D	O	L	A	R

NOTE: The cartoon figure is the versatile Donizetti, shown writing tragedy with his left hand and comedy with his right – an envoi to all the opera fans who, with similar versatility, diverted themselves with these puzzles.

FATHER LEE